CUMBRIA
LIBRARIES

COUNTY COUNCIL
This book is due to be returned on
may be renewed by personal applicat
demand.

C.L.18

Churchill: Visionary. Statesman. Historian.

John Lukacs

Churchill: Visionary. Statesman. Historian.

YALE UNIVERSITY PRESS

NEW HAVEN & LONDON

Parts (rewritten) of Chapters 3, 4, 7, and 8 appeared in *The New Yorker* (1985), in *The New York Times Book Review* (1991), in *The Washington Post* (1993), and in the London *Spectator* (2001). The last chapter appeared in *Destinations Past* (University of Missouri Press, 1994). All reprinted material used with permission.

Designed by Nancy Ovedovitz and set in Postscript Didot type by Achorn Graphic Services. Printed in the United States of America by R. R. Donnelley & Sons.

Library of Congress Cataloging-in-Publication Data
Lukacs, John, 1924–
Churchill : visionary, statesman, historian / John Lukacs.
p. cm.
Includes bibliographical references (p.   ) and index.
ISBN 0-300-09769-7 (cloth : alk. paper)
1. Churchill, Winston, Sir, 1874–1965. 2. Great Britain — Politics and government — 20th century. 3. Prime ministers — Great Britain — Biography. 4. Historians — Great Britain — Biography.
I. Title.

DA566.9.C5 L85 2002
941.084′092 — dc21   2002069147
[B]

A catalogue record for this book is available from the British Library.

The paper in this book meets the guidelines for permanence and durability of the Committee on Production Guidelines for Book Longevity of the Council on Library Resources.

10   9   8   7   6   5   4   3   2   1

For
M. S.

I earnestly trust that only those will
read it who really wish to do so.
—Last sentence of the Preface to
The Groombridge Diary

Contents

Preface

In these first years of the twenty-first century Winston Churchill's reputation is at a peak. Why this is so I cannot really explain. After all, nearly forty years have now gone since his death, and nearly fifty years since the end of his public career. Of course his image has gained from perspective: he looms large in contrast to the many mediocrities who have occupied or flitted through the stages of world politics since his time. At times I think that there is another element. More than a decade after the collapse of the Soviet Union we can see that between the two monstrous adversaries of the West during the twentieth century the Soviet Union was weaker, and Hitler's Third Reich was stronger, than people were accustomed to think; and was it not Churchill who, at the direst moments of the Second World War, stood up against a Hitler who had come very close to winning it? (But then such a perspective would occur only to those who lived through the war or who have thought much about that . . .) In any event: recent evidences of admiration for Churchill are often surprising. After a handful of fanatic Arabs drove hijacked airplanes into the

two high towers of New York, some people invoked Churchill's name and courage during the Blitz – yet the Blitz was
something quite different. I have been amused as well as irritated by recent appearances of speakers addressing various
Churchill Society meetings, persons who not many years before had disparaged him in print; and also one or two who in
1940 had been adamant opponents of any kind of American
aid to Britain, especially to a Britain led by Churchill the warmonger. There *was* a lull in Churchilliana in the 1980s, at the
end of which the first massive criticisms of Churchill by some
historians were published; but the tide of his renown rose
again. Only last year two important biographies of Churchill
appeared (see Chapter 8). In January 2001, too, a conference
at the Institute of Historical Research in the University of London was titled "Churchill in the Twenty-First Century"; its
papers were published in *Transactions of the Royal Historical
Society*, series 6, vol. XI, at the end of the year. It may be significant that among the fifteen scholars and public personalities who participated only one historian was severely critical
of Churchill. (Another's criticism was more balanced. References to both may be found in Chapters 3 and 7.)

Historians may now avail themselves of the vast and superbly catalogued Churchill Archives in Cambridge (lodged in
a dreadfully ugly modern pile of a building, alas). But the extent of Churchill materials is vast, far beyond that rich collection. I too have been a beneficiary of the recent interest in
Churchill: two books of mine, one published at the beginning
and the other at the end of the 1990s, reconstructions of
Churchill during the most dangerous and crucial months and

days of 1940, received favorable reviews and surprisingly many buyers and readers not only in the English-speaking countries of the world but also elsewhere. This present small volume is neither a biography nor a scholarly study of Churchill's life, though it rests on a lifetime of study and reading. Its contents may illuminate some little-known or unappreciated aspects of Churchill and suggest some subjects that have not yet been fully explored, even in the mass of literature about him; thus some of these perspectives (or arguments) include suggestions for further research. Another limitation is my frequent emphasis on Churchill's role during the Second World War and after. But of course 1940 was the great dividing line in his career. Before 1940 he had many a failure; he made many mistakes. Then in 1940 he was the man who did not lose the Second World War. That had inspired me then; it still inspires me now. In an essay about Churchill's historianship (see Chapter 6) J. C. Plumb wrote that "the past in which [Churchill] believed" is lost. "What gave Churchill his confidence, his courage, his burning faith in the rightness of his cause — his deep sense of the miraculous English past — has been lost." I know what Plumb meant. Still . . . I do not *quite* believe this.

2001–2002

Churchill: Visionary. Statesman. Historian.

1

Churchill the visionary

It is one of the oddities of the English language—and of the sensitivities of the English mind—that while the word *vision* is commendatory, suggesting a positive quality, *visionary* may have, indeed often does have, a dubious sense. There are of course varieties of the meanings of these words in the *Oxford English Dictionary*, but here are at least the principal ones. *Vision:* "Something which is apparently seen otherwise than by ordinary sight," or "A mental concept of a distinct and vivid kind: a highly imaginative scheme or anticipation." On the other hand, *Visionary:* "Given to fanciful and unpractical views; speculative, dreamy," or "Existing in imagination only; not actual or real," or "One who indulges in fantastic ideas or schemes; an unpractical enthusiast." This last pejorative meaning, according to the *OED*, appears in English in 1702. Two and a quarter centuries later this was how Winston Churchill's English opponents—and many others, too—saw him. But it is not with opponents and critics of Churchill that I am here concerned. My purpose in this chapter is different.

It is to assert that *visionary* may be properly and, I hope, convincingly, applicable to Churchill in a positive sense.

He was extraordinary — well and good; but there is more to that. There was no one else who could have done what he did in 1940. This is a matter that, after more than sixty years, we ought to see somewhat differently from how we saw it for a long time. In 1940 Churchill, alone, stood across the path of Hitler's victory. Not only Americans — who, justifiably, associate the start of their Second World War with December 1941 — but many other people, including serious historians and biographers of Hitler, tend to see Hitler as having been doomed by a war that he started and in which he and his Reich would be overwhelmed by the associated might of Britain, the United States, and the Soviet Union. But what few people understand is how close Hitler had come to winning his war in the early summer of 1940, and well before the air Battle of Britain. He would have won his war if he had sent a small German army to land in England in June or July — that much has been recognized by a few, mostly British, military historians. But that is a speculation. What is not a speculation is what Churchill, on the twenty-seventh of May in 1940, in the secret sessions of the War Cabinet, called "the slippery slope." If at that time a British government had signaled as much as a cautious inclination to explore a negotiation with Hitler, amounting to a willingness to ascertain his possible terms, that would have been the first step onto a Slippery Slope from which there could be no retreat. There were people who did not see eye to eye with Churchill about that: beyond the secrecy of the War Cabinet room there were many of the Conservative Party; and perhaps there was the majority of the elected representatives of the British people, of the Conservative Party; and there was at least the potentiality that, under different circumstances, the manhood and the womanhood of Britain may have consented to such an, at least seemingly, reasonable and prudent course. But Churchill did not let go; and he had his way. That was the greatest turning point — a turning point, more than a milestone — in his career. It may have been the greatest turning point in the history of the Second World War. During the succeeding months Churchill and Britain defied Hitler's Third Reich almost alone. Later he was no longer alone. He and his Britain could not conquer Hitler by themselves; but as long as Churchill governed Britain, Hitler could not win his war. Probably this was the reason why Hitler's hatred for Churchill burned so fiercely till the very end. Hitler respected and even admired Stalin; he spoke contemptuously of Roosevelt; but his hatred for Churchill flared in his mind above the others.

But the bravery and the resolution that Churchill demonstrated at that time were inseparable from certain elements of his vision. Visionary elements may be recognizable also at other times of his career. Some of these elements may be more obvious than are others. As early as 1901 he said in Parliament: "Democracy is more vindictive than Cabinets. The wars of peoples will be more terrible than those of kings." (Note that he said this at a time when predictions about the impracticability of great future wars were current among many political thinkers.) Even more stunning — and daunting — is what this, very young Churchill wrote in the twenty-fifth year of his life, in *The River War:* "I hope that if evil days should come upon our country, and the last army which a collapsing Empire could interpose between London and the invader was dissolving in rout and ruin, that there would be some — even in these modern days — who would not care to accustom themselves to the new order of things and tamely survive the disaster."* Now one last glance at the meaning of the word *visionary.* In every sense — whether good or bad — the word suggests foresight. Now foresight may be bad as well as good, excessive as well as inadequate — note that characteristically British proverb: "We'll cross that bridge when we get to it." That admonition invokes the pragmatism of common sense; but it may also lead to an unwillingness to think too much, or too fast. Only a few years before 1940 Churchill's predecessor Prime Minister Stanley Baldwin was supposed to have said: "The man who says he can see far ahead is a charlatan." (He did not mean Churchill.) As Robert Rhodes James wrote: "Foresight in politics is rare, and it is usually a matter of fortune rather than genius."† Perhaps; but, at any rate, Churchill's foresights were historical rather than political. Impetuosity, impatience, willfulness, fancifulness were Churchill's faults, often. Shortsightedness? No. An unwillingness to think? Seldom: perhaps never. He had an extraordinarily quick mind, and these traits of his were not only inseparable from his temperament and

* Cited by Maurice Ashley, *Churchill as Historian,* New York, 1968, p. 49.

† Robert Rhodes James, *Churchill: A Study in Failure, 1900–1939,* New York, 1971, p. 381.

character but inseparable, too, from the visionary capacity of his mind.

One example of this was his visionary assessment of Hitler and of his Third Reich. That during the crucial summer months of 1940 Churchill understood Hitler better than Hitler understood him was a great asset. (Note, too, that this kind of intelligent human understanding at that time had almost nothing to do with the later so-celebrated British intelligence interception and reading of German signals and codes.) The struggle between Churchill and Hitler during those months was a veritable duel — the title that I chose for my book dealing with those eighty days, describing the two leaders' reciprocal moves, among other things. But there was more involved here than the fact of one strategist besting the other. A chess master is a superb calculator, perhaps even a strategist: but a visionary he is not. Yet Churchill's understanding of his great opponent contained insights that could be properly recognized as visionary ones.

He — better than the French, whose post-1918 view of Germany was a combination of myopia and fear: and fear will not a clear vision make — foresaw the rise of a revengeful Germany as early as 1924: "The enormous contingents of German youth growing to military manhood year by year are inspired by the fiercest sentiments, and the soul of Germany smoulders with dreams of a war of liberation or revenge." He looked well beyond the fevers of cosmopolitan Berlin or those of the parliament of the Weimar Republic; he espied another fever, that of the then still small bands of storm troopers, marching through German towns or banging their beer mugs in Bavarian halls.

In October 1930 Churchill dined at the German embassy in London. He said at the table that he was anxious about Hitler. The Counselor of the Embassy, a descendant of Bismarck, considered Churchill's words significant enough to report them to Berlin. They may be found in the collection of German diplomatic documents. Note that this happened in 1930, at a time when no one — certainly no one in England, but also no one in Germany, perhaps with the exception of Hitler himself — thought that Hitler could ever become the Chancellor and leader of the German nation. In July 1932 Churchill wrote that Hitler was "the moving impulse below the German government and may be more than that soon." So he was to be.

But even more visionary was what Churchill wrote about Hitler and Germany in early 1935.* When Germany had been defeated, collapsed, in the throes of revolution, disarmed, "then [in 1919] it was that one corporal, a former Austrian house-painter,† set out to regain all."

In the fifteen years that have followed this resolve he has succeeded in restoring Germany to the most powerful position in Europe, and not only has he restored the position of his country, but he has even, to a very large extent, reversed the results of the Great War. . . . [Now] the vanquished are in process of becoming the victors, and the victors the vanquished. When Hitler began, Germany lay

*There is at least some indication that he wrote it as early as 1934. It was reprinted in *Great Contemporaries*, London, 1937, p. 262.

†Hitler had painted pictures of houses, but he was not a house-painter.

prostrate at the feet of the Allies. He may yet see the day
when what is left of Europe will be prostrate at the feet of
Germany. Whatever else may be thought about these ex-
ploits, they are certainly among the most remarkable in the
whole history of the world.

Whatever else may be thought about these words, they are certainly among the most remarkable – and accurate – forecasts
in the history of the origins of the Second World War. And
in early 1935, when Churchill was all alone. No one else saw
such a prospect then, not even the most pessimistic adversaries of Hitler. But then Churchill never underestimated Hitler.

Thereafter, during the late Thirties, we have a long series
of Churchill's comments about Hitler, some of which are well-
known. Some of them are more pertinent than are others, but
they are always interesting and telling. But let me now jump
ahead and bring up another instance that has fascinated me
for a long time. This is a brief sketch of Hitler's character that
Churchill dictated in 1948 when he composed the first volume
of his War Memoirs. There he said that the crystallization of
Hitler's view of the world occurred not before the First World
War but in 1919; and not in Vienna but in Munich. Yet Hitler
in *Mein Kampf* had insisted – and most historians have accepted the thesis – that while his life took a turn in 1918–1919 in
Munich, his political ideology had crystallized in Vienna about
eight or nine years earlier. Well, about fifty years after 1948 a
few historians (including myself but especially the excellent
Brigitte Hamann, in Vienna) have been revising the Vienna
thesis, fortified by evidence which includes Hitler's conscious
misstating the sequence of the evolution of his ideas. Yet fifty

years earlier, in those rapidly dictated pages, Churchill's insight into the young Hitler was phenomenal.

Churchill's view — and sometimes, indeed, his vision — of the destiny of the German people was not simple. Many people, especially in Germany, have seen (and still see) Churchill as a representation of an atavistic Germanophobe Britisher, an old-fashioned John Bull, obsessed with the spectre of German power and obsessed with a single-minded desire to destroy it. Yet — all of those famous bulldoglike Karsh photographs notwithstanding — Churchill was not a reincarnation of John Bull, not in his personality, in his character, or in his wide interest and knowledge of the world beyond England. What I must mention here are the many evidences of Churchill's respect for Germany and its people. They are there, forcefully expressed in the last passages of *World Crisis*, his history of the First World War; they may be found in the last volume of his Second World War memoirs when, visiting a ruined Berlin in the summer of 1945, he writes about himself that now he had nothing but sympathy for the ragged and hungry people he saw;* and there is his 1946 address in Zurich, nearly equal in importance to his Iron Curtain speech in Fulton, Missouri, in that year, in which he exhorted France and Germany to form a new kind of alliance, in order to begin a new chapter in the evolving history of Western Europe. Less evident but more latent there was his increasing recognition during the war of

* Contrast this with Patrick J. Buchanan: "By 1945 Germany had been destroyed and Churchill could poke about its ruins." *A Republic, Not an Empire*, Washington, 1999, p. 275.

what the Germans were able to accomplish, of how formidable their armies were. There are reasons to believe, and some evidence, that after El Alamein he kept impressing Field Marshal Montgomery with that. This brings me to another example of his visionary quality that I have often cited. He saw that Hitler had forged a formidable unity of a people; that German National Socialism was a terrific wave of a possible future; and it was against this that his Britain had to stand fast. Consider, in this respect, the difference between Churchill's vision and that of the French premier, Paul Reynaud. In June 1940, a few days before Paris fell, Reynaud broadcast to the French people: If Hitler wins this war, "it would be the Middle Ages again, but not illuminated by the mercy of Christ." A few days later, on 18 June, in his "Finest Hour" speech Churchill saw a very different prospect—not a return to the Middle Ages but a lurch into a New Dark Age. If Hitler wins and we fall, he said, "then the whole world, including the United States, including all that we have known and care for, will sink into the abyss of a New Dark Age, made more sinister, and perhaps more protracted, by the lights of perverted science." Note the word "protracted." He, better than Reynaud, and perhaps better than anyone else, knew what he had to stand against.

I am coming now to another instance: to Churchill's view of Europe—which, again, shows him as someone different from the type of John Bull. John Bull was single-minded. Winston Churchill was not. There are dualities in the inclinations of most human beings. One of Churchill's dualities in his vision of the world and of its history involved England's relationship to the United States (and to the English-speaking peoples) on the one hand, and to Europe on the other. His sense of the Anglo-European relationship is a rich and complex theme. It involves, among other things, his great appreciation for the civilization and culture of Europe, together with his respect for its ancient constituents, such as the constitutional monarchies that were still the principal forms of state in his lifetime. (Note that as late as in the thirty-sixth year of his life there were only two republics in all of Europe: France and Switzerland.) But it would be wrong to attribute Churchill's view of Europe to the attraction of Victorian or even Edwardian memories in his mind. Nor was his Francophilia the logical consequence of the Germanophobia of which he has been often accused. His affection for French culture and civilization and history (consider only his often expressed admiration for Joan of Arc and his respect for Napoleon) went deeper than that.

But then here I come to the perhaps narrow but essentially deep difference that separated Churchill from most of his contemporaries in the Conservative Party of his time. They knew less of Europe than Churchill; more important, they were more suspicious of English ties and commitments to Europe than was Churchill. They did not comprehend the awesome dimensions of Hitler's purposes and of his power, while they took some comfort from his anti-Communism. At the same time they did not understand that if Britain allowed Germany to dominate all of Central and most of Eastern Europe, the independence of Western Europe, including France, would be fatefully compromised and fatefully constrained; that what was at stake was more than the traditional questions of a balance of power. There were, and there still are, many German, some American, Eastern European, and lately even British historians who criticize Churchill for having pursued his policy of fighting Germany, with the result that the destruction of German power led to the presence of Russian power in the eastern half of the Continent. Yet this melancholy outcome of the Second World War in Europe was not an outcome of some kind of Churchillian shortsightedness. Thus I arrive at another example of his visionary capacities: to his view of Russia during the war — and not only during the war. My purpose here is not to argue in favor of his statesmanship in terms of political realism, except to argue something that I must also repeat elsewhere in this book (while history does not repeat itself, historians sometimes do . . .), which is what I have long seen as the essence of Winston Churchill's statesmanship in the Second World War. As early as 1940 he saw two alternatives: either Germany dominates all of Europe; or Russia will dominate the eastern portion of Europe (at worst for a while): and half of Europe is better than none. I shall come to his relationship with Stalin in the next chapter: of his attempt to understand Stalin, of his constraints, of his knowledge that without Russia Germany might be unconquerable. But here I wish to refer not to Churchill's pragmatism but to his visionary capacities. One instance of this may be his famous remark to his secretary a few hours before his great speech of 22 June 1941, the evening of the day when Germany invaded Russia — a remark, at first sight perhaps somewhat frivolous, that he characteristically felt proper to record in his War Memoirs: "If Hitler invaded Hell I would at least make a favourable reference to the Devil in the House of Commons."* That realization that The Opponent Of My Enemy May Be My Ally is the reaction of a pragmatist statesman — but I am interested in more than that. I am interested in Churchill's recognition that Stalin was a nationalist and not an Internationalist Communist; and that the clue to the Russian "enigma" lay in the interests of the Russian imperial state as seen by Stalin. His understanding of Stalin explains his, sometimes criticized, agreements with the Soviet leader, including the 1944 Percentages Agreement, through which Churchill succeeded in saving Greece (and which Stalin rather meticulously kept).

And it was Churchill's vision of a postwar Russian danger that lay behind his futile urgings to design Anglo-American strategy in the last year of the war with the purpose of arriving as far east in Central Europe as was possible, in order to forestall a dangerous extension of Russian military presence there. This had little to do with Communism, but it had everything to do with where the Russian and the Anglo-American armies would meet and stand at the end of the war — in essence, where the division line across Europe would occur and what it would mean. That was the essence of his Iron Curtain speech in Fulton too. From 1943 to 1946 Churchill encountered criticisms and misunderstandings from many

---

*I once found a forerunner of that phrase; I wonder whether Churchill had been aware of it. In the Irish nationalist paper *Fianna* Dr. Eoin McNeill wrote in September 1915 (note that this was published in Dublin in the midst of the First World War): "If Hell itself were to turn against English policy, as it is known to us, we might be pardoned for taking the side of Hell."

Americans, who thought — and at least suggested openly, on occasion — that Churchill's ideas reflected views that were narrowly British, imperialist, reactionary, and dangerously anti-Russian. Recall, too, that even the Fulton speech was very cautiously treated by Washington, with courteous disavowals and a few private approvals, while it was openly attacked by politicians and the press, and by the American Right as well as by the American Left.

It now may be said — and, I admit, with a certain amount of cogency — that, perhaps contrary to my earlier distinction, what I have just made were arguments attempting to portray Churchill the pragmatist rather than Churchill the visionary. Yet such a distinctive caveat cannot be applied to his long-range vision of the future of Europe and of Communism, evidences of which are extant. It is remarkable that he chose to entitle the last volume of his War Memoirs *Triumph and Tragedy*, because of the unnatural division of Europe and the coming of the cold war — while no such usage of the word *tragedy* may be found in the war memoirs or assessments of Americans or Russians of that time. It is remarkable that the entire second part of this volume bears the title "The Iron Curtain." It is remarkable, too, and amply proved, that Churchill chose to underemphasize, indeed to eliminate, many of his records and recollections of his misunderstandings with American political and military leaders in 1944–1945, for pragmatic reasons, since that volume was about to be published at a time when his wartime ally Eisenhower was about to become the president of the United States; and surely also because of Churchill's magnanimity, his characteristic unwillingness to remind people: "I told you so." But the nature of his vision — in this case verily meaning foresight — appears from two sources. One is in General de Gaulle's memoirs. Churchill returned to Paris after four years, in November 1944. It was a memorable occasion. He cried. And when General de Gaulle criticized the Americans who were letting so much of Eastern Europe go to the Russians, Churchill answered that, yes, this was so; Russia was now a big hungry wolf, in the midst of sheep; but after the meal comes the digestion period. Russia will not be able to digest what she was now about to swallow. The second instance is the remark he dropped to John Colville, on New Year's Day in 1953 (consider that this was said even before Stalin's death): "(Churchill) said that if I lived my normal span I should assuredly see Eastern Europe free of Communism." Counting Colville's expectable threescore and ten, that would have been the 1980s — which was exactly what happened. Bismarck was reputed to have said that a statesman can look forward five years, at best. It is given to few statesmen in history to suggest the unexpected, decades ahead, so accurately and clearly. Yet such were the visionary powers of Winston Churchill.

He was astonishingly right about Hitler. He was largely right about Communism and Stalin. About the first he was able to translate his views into action. About the second — because of many constraints and also because of American unwillingness — only partly so. He also believed that the American idea of anticolonialism was, at least partly, premature. He did not share the frequent American inclination of considering China as a Great Power. Yes, he was an imperialist; yes, he did say —

at one, fateful occasion, in one, fateful phrase — that he had
not become Prime Minister to preside over the liquidation of
the British Empire.* We cannot say what would have happened with the Empire had he remained Prime Minister after
July 1945. I am inclined to think that, except here and there,
the ending of the Empire would not have been altogether different. What I can say is that his vision of Europe and his vision of the Anglo-American relationship were clearer than any
vision he still may have had about the future of the Empire.

And here I arrive at — and conclude with — a summary of his
protracted vision (and perhaps of his greatest failure): that of
an eventual confederation of the English-speaking peoples of
the world. He possessed this vision from the very beginning
to the very end of his public life — from his youthful support
of his mother who published a short-lived *Anglo-Saxon Review*
from 1899 to 1901 (Churchill did not like the title) through liter-
ally innumerable printed and spoken instances, culminating
in the final publication of his four volumes of *The History of
the English-Speaking Peoples* in the second half of the 1950s.
His affection and respect for the United States was attributable
to more than the influence of his American-born mother.

* One of Churchill's greatest failures, harming his reputation and
his career, was that of his strident opposition to granting Dominion
status to India, 1929 to 1935: "Once we lose confidence in our mission
in the East, once we repudiate our responsibilities to foreigners and
minorities, once we feel ourselves unable calmly and fearlessly to dis-
charge our duties to vast helpless populations, then our presence in
these countries will be stripped of every moral sanction." (Cited in
James, *Churchill*, p. 218.) And was he entirely wrong?

It included his vision of the future of the world. It was historic
more than racial, civilizational more than cultural, with one of
its fundaments being the quality of his interest in and the extent of his knowledge of American history. Let me mention
but one, interesting and perhaps even inspiring, item. In a delightful little book entitled *If* (Subtitle: "If It Had Happened
Otherwise / Lapses into Imaginary History"), edited by J. C.
Squire in 1931, Churchill contributed a chapter which reversed
the logic and the order of all the other chapters. Those chapters had such titles as "If Napoleon Had Not Lost at Waterloo."
But Churchill's chapter bore the title "If Lee Had Not Won the
Battle of Gettysburg." In this brilliant *tour de force* Churchill
speculated about the regrettable consequences of Lee's imag-
ined defeat at Gettysburg — for then, alas, the rapid ending of
the War Between the States, and the American confederation
with the other English-speaking nations of the world would
not have happened, and the lamentable result would have
been a First World War. So this was but another summary
expression of Churchill's vision: had there been a closer
union, perhaps even a federation, of the United States and of
the English-speaking countries of the world, the First and
then the Second World War could never have occurred; the
world would have entered another Age of the Antonines, moving forward to the sunny uplands of a democratic world order,
buttressed by the mild and benevolent global and maritime
primacy of the English-speaking peoples.

   We ought to consider that this vision was not devoid of reality — by which I mean the potentiality of its accomplishment. It
was exactly after 1895 that the American inclination for Twist-

ing the Lion's Tail began to disappear; and after 1900 the idea
of a Pax Britannica was being replaced in the minds of some
very acute people by the image of a Pax Anglo-Americana.
This was not only a governing idea of Churchill during much
of his public life, from about 1895 to 1955. It corresponded, at
least for some time, with the inclinations of some people
among the American upper classes. It is at least possible that
Churchill may have been unduly influenced by his connections and contacts with such people, that he was insufficiently
aware how the composition and the structure of the American
population were changing, and that consequently the influences of an Anglophile leading class were lessening. Perhaps
he recognized this; perhaps not. In any event: *this* vision of a
closer and closer union of the English-speaking peoples of the
world was not to be.

And now I end this chapter about Churchill's vision with a
suggestion about his place in history. These matters are connected. Contrary to most accepted views we ought to consider
that he was not some kind of admirable remnant of a more
heroic past. He was not The Last Lion. He was something else.
He represented certain aristocratic traits in an age of democracy that he felt bound to accept and eventually cherish. He
knew that not only the primacy of his nation among world
powers but perhaps an entire era in the world that had begun
about four hundred years before his birth was moving toward
its end. In sum, he was the defender of civilization at the end
of the Modern Age. That word, *civilization,* also appeared first
in English five hundred years ago, defined then as the antithesis of barbarism. At a dramatic moment in the twentieth cen-

tury God allowed Churchill the task of being its principal defender. And now one more startling and stunning example of his visionary quality. He was old and weary, in poor health, when in 1955 he felt compelled to end his public life. Yet in his last speech in the House of Commons in 1955 he, as one of his recent biographers writes,* said something "unforgettable . . . which illuminated the dreadful prospect like a sheet of lightning" — about the ending of our world. Churchill said: "Which way shall we turn to save our lives and the future of the world? It does not matter so much for old people; they are going soon anyway; but I find it poignant to look at youth in all its activity and ardour . . . and wonder what would lie before them *if God wearied of mankind?*" Churchill was not a religious man: but this was a bourdon bell of foreboding, as from the heart and mouth of an Old Testament visionary and prophet.

Readers of this — in some ways introductory — chapter ought not mistake its purpose, which is a summation neither of Churchill's virtues nor of his career. It arises from a conception of the historian's task which is not only to give a precise account of persons or of periods but to point out and to consider problems: problems of our understanding of places and people in the past, as well as the problem of the dualities of certain persons. To a description of such problems of Churchill's life, to wit: his relations with Stalin; with Roosevelt; with Eisenhower; with Europe; his historianship; his failures and his critics, I shall now turn.

* In Roy Jenkins, *Churchill*, New York, 2001, p. 893.

2

Churchill and Stalin

There is a chapter in the second volume of Tocqueville's *Democracy in America* that has seldom (if ever) attracted the attention it deserves. It is hardly longer than a page and a half; it contains not more than forty-eight sentences. It is entitled "Some Characteristics of Historians in Democratic Times." I have often thought that it ought perhaps be framed and put above every working historian's and history student's desk. For Tocqueville's sentences tell us that the writing of history in the age of democracy, in the age ruled by sovereign majorities, will be more difficult than and different from the writing of history in ages ruled by aristocratic minorities. And he foresaw, too, that historians in a democratic age will tend to be preoccupied with great general movements of societies and ideas, with the attendant tendency to neglect the motives, acts, and purposes of significant persons.

Yet even in democratic times the course of the histories of entire nations may depend on outstanding personalities. This applies to the Second World War more than to almost any great event or period of history during the past two hundred years. Hitler, Churchill, Stalin, Roosevelt, de Gaulle (to a lesser extent even Mussolini): without them not only the course of that enormous war but its origins, its outbreak, its turning points, and its outcome would not only have been entirely different: much of it would not have happened at all. These leaders were living proofs that apart from, or perhaps even contrary to, the idea that history consists of large economic and social movements, to understand the history of that time we must primarily (but of course not exclusively) concentrate on the acts and the relations of a few great national leaders.

Churchill, Stalin, Roosevelt: they won the Second World War. (In one sense, Churchill was *the* key figure, because in 1940 he was the man who did not lose it — for that was the moment when Hitler could have won the war. After Russia and America became involved, Hitler could no longer win, even though he — and this is still far from being adequately understood — could have forced his adversaries to something like a draw.) Churchill, Stalin, Roosevelt — they were very different men: but here my purpose is a description and analysis not of their characters but of their relations: and in view not only of the Second World War but also of its enormous consequences. For those consequences not only influenced but determined the history of the world at least for fifty years. The two world wars were the two great mountain ranges that towered over the landscape of an entire century. The cold war, from 1947 to 1989, was the direct consequence of the Second World War — that is, something other than the much-touted world struggle between Communism and capitalism, or between Communism and "freedom." And the origins of the cold war depended on and had issued from the relations of Churchill and Stalin and Roosevelt.

About these triangular relationships much material has accumulated and much has been written during the past sixty years, much about Churchill-Roosevelt, less about Roosevelt-Stalin, and less about Churchill-Stalin. Yet that last relationship, including their two summit meetings, may have been the most decisive one, at least for Europe and its then future.

Historical thinking and writing and study are, by their nature, revisionist. The historian, unlike a judge, is permitted to try a case over and over again, often after finding and employing new evidence. Now, despite the disordered trickle of documents seeping out from Russian archives during the past dozen years or so, there seems to be not much reason to believe (or hope) that they could provide evidence to revise not only the essentials but even the details of the Churchill-Stalin relationship. Yet the human mind includes the capacity as well as the inclination to rethink much of the past, over and over — and not necessarily because of new evidence but because of changing perspectives: and perspective is, of course, an inevitable component of the act of seeing.

Much of the written (and, on occasion, spoken) criticism of Churchill has been directed at his treatment of Stalin (and of Soviet Russia) during the Second World War. The personal and political inclinations of his critics may differ, but the essence of their criticism is the same. They accuse Churchill of double standards. He, who fought bitterly and single-mindedly against the appeasement of Germany and of Hitler, went a very long way to appease Stalin and Russia. He had no illusions about Hitler, but nurtured — and expressed — many an unwarranted illusion about Stalin. His hatred of Germany blinded him throughout the war. It also made him an accomplice in allowing Russia and Communism to advance far into the heart of Europe. (Such criticism is often apparent among German historians and certain journalists, including men and women who cannot be accused of nurturing sympathies for Hitler.) He, who had attacked his own government for abandoning Czechoslovakia to Germany, abandoned Poland to Russia. (It is interesting that the latter criticism has been voiced less often by Polish than by non-Polish historians and writers.)

There is *some* substance in these criticisms, even when they are ideological or national or exaggeratedly one-sided. Yet almost none of Churchill's critics consider an essential condition, which was the need to keep up the alliance with Soviet Russia, without which Britain and the United States could hardly — or perhaps not at all — have expected to conquer Germany. However: neither the scope nor the purpose of this chapter concern primarily British-Russian relations during the war. They concern the minds and the relationships of the two leaders, Churchill and Stalin.

Churchill's view of Stalin was not simple. It contained elements of illusion; but also of a supreme (and — if I may so say, old-fashioned) realism. Eventually his view and treatment of Stalin became entirely separate from his view and treatment of Communism. Even before the war he began to see Russia and its leader as a national, and not an ideological, reality. We do not know whether Churchill heard the witticism of the English wag who upon the news of the Nazi-Soviet (and Hitler-Stalin) Pact in 1939 said that "All the Isms are Wasms," but there is at least reason to think that Churchill would have chuckled at it. He of course abhorred Communism from the very beginning. His strenuous advocacy of Allied intervention in the Russian civil war in 1919–1920 was more than yet another instance of his romantic pugnacity. He believed that the Bolsheviks were weak enough so that a little more Allied help to their White Russian opponents would topple them: but if not, they would remain and grow into a serious threat to other nations of the world. Anti-Communism was one (though only one) of his reasons to esteem Mussolini and other European (and Asian) anti-Communist dictators and leaders. His contempt for Communism did not lessen. One example of this was his preference for the Franco side at the beginning of and for some time during the Spanish civil war, for a number of reasons, among them the presence of Communists in the Left-inclined republican regime in Madrid.

However — and this is important — Hitler's declared "conservative" anti-Communism, which in the 1930s was extremely successful, bringing and ranging entire classes of people and nations to the German side, made no impression on Churchill, who was then a minority among conservatives. He saw through the propaganda of the Third Reich, including the Anti-Comintern Pact; he saw the danger of a new Germany, rising and arming. Consequently he began to give some consideration (as had the French government, beginning in 1934) to the possibility of Soviet Russia's eventually becoming part of an anti-German alliance of states, perhaps in the name of "collective security." Whether already at that time Churchill saw Stalin as more and more of a national and less and less of an international revolutionary leader we cannot tell. What we can tell is that his view of Communism and his view of Russia began to diverge. He, the known right-wing imperialist who fought against granting Dominion status to India, and thereafter for more and more British armament, now found himself supported by more and more people on the "Left." His circle of acquaintances now also included the Soviet Russian ambassador to London, Ivan Maisky, a sly politic personage who (as we now know from the texts of his dispatches to Moscow) does not deserve the reputation he had acquired but who knew how to say some things that Churchill liked to hear.

Yet Churchill, who saw Hitler and his purposes perhaps better than any other statesman in the world, especially in 1938–1939, was wrong about Russia, and especially about Stalin at that time. People did not know it then; we know (or at least ought to know) it now. Before and during the Munich crisis Churchill believed, and argued, that Hitler's Germany had to be resisted and, if necessary, fought then and there, for many reasons, including Russia's participation in such a war: after all, Russia had an alliance with France and with Czechoslovakia at that time. Ten years later he repeated his argument, directly and powerfully, in *The Gathering Storm*, the first volume of his Second World War history. He should have known already then what became more and more evident later: that in September 1938 Stalin had no more (indeed, even less) intention to honor his alliance with Czechoslovakia than had the

French; indeed, that Stalin was pleased to get off the hook (if indeed hook that was).

I shall have to say something about Churchill around Munich, about his then-compound of realism and illusions, in another chapter; but here my purpose is to reconstruct the compound of his realism and his illusions about Stalin. Well after Munich he continued to believe that a British-French alliance with Russia was absolutely essential to deter Hitler. After March 1939 he was no longer alone in pushing for this; and in regretting that the Chamberlain government was both dilatory and reluctant in pursuing a serious military alliance with Soviet Russia he was probably right. Yet he was wrong in thinking that Stalin was willing to enter into such an alliance at all. Considerable evidence indicates that in 1939 (as well as later) Stalin preferred to cut a deal with Hitler rather than with the Western capitalist democracies. And so it happened. There is some reason to believe that, stunned as he was, like almost everyone else, Churchill was less shocked by the Stalin-Hitler Pact than were many others. It was on 1 October 1939 — he was already a member of the Chamberlain cabinet then — that he uttered his later famous sentences: "I cannot forecast to you the action of Russia. It is a riddle wrapped in a mystery inside an enigma: but perhaps there is a key. That key is Russian national interest." (Chamberlain, whose disgust with the Soviets was more fundamental than Churchill's, wrote to him that he entirely agreed.)

Russian national interest — something very different, and definitely more important, than International Communism — Churchill was right about that then, and ever since. I must insist on this even now, more than a decade after the collapse of Communism and of the Soviet Union. Both before and during the cold war there were (and there still are) entire governments and peoples who saw the entire history of the twentieth century governed by a tremendous struggle between International Communism and The Free World (whatever that is). Of course Russia was a Communist state, and Moscow still the capital city of International Communism: but the latter was subordinated to Russia's national interests — or, more precisely: to what Stalin saw as those interests — well before 1939, and certainly after. Churchill understood that; as a matter of fact, perhaps he understood it *too well*. He saw Stalin as a national dictator: a brutal and cynical leader but a statesman nevertheless. We shall soon see that, especially after 1941, that element of romantic sentimentality which may be inherent in many instances of a visionary capacity carried Churchill too far, when he felt a need to express his high esteem for Stalin on occasion. But before proceeding to their personal relations let me say something about Churchill's conviction: that, Communism notwithstanding, Russian national interest might not be irreconcilable with Britain's. For there was a consistency that ran like a red thread through Churchill's vision of the world from 1939 till practically the end of his life. It was there in 1939 when he sought an alliance with Stalin's Russia; it was there in 1939 and 1940 when Stalin was practically allied with Hitler; it was there in 1941 and after when Churchill and Stalin became allies; it was there throughout and especially toward the end of the war when he saw Stalin's Russia as a great and present danger; it was there in and after 1945 when he warned

Americans and the world about that danger and insisted on
the necessity of resisting and opposing it; it was there in 1952
and after when he attempted, in vain, to renegotiate the division of Europe, which was the essence of the cold war, with
the Russians. This was that Russia's national interests must
be seriously considered — though defined and kept within reasonable limits, whenever possible. And here we must consider
that, from all evidence, most of British political and public and
popular opinion about a potential concordance of British and
Russian interests accorded with Churchill's view in 1939–1941
as well as in 1941–1945.*

There is no need here to describe, or perhaps even to sum
up, British-Russian relations before Hitler's invasion of Russia, even though they include Churchill's letter to Stalin written after the fall of France, a great state paper, read but dismissed by Stalin; and then Churchill's insistent — and again
consistently, suspiciously, contemptibly disregarded — indi-
rect and direct warnings to Stalin from April to June 1941 about
the impending German invasion. So now we come to their uneasy but nonetheless de facto alliance, starting on that very
Sunday, 22 June, which was Stalin's worst day, but not
Churchill's, not in the least. Broadcast at nine that night he
made one of his great speeches, the sum of which was that
while he renounced nothing that he had said about Commu-

* One example: an editorial in the *Times* of London on 1 August 1941:
"Leadership in Eastern Europe can only fall to Germany or Russia.
Neither Great Britain nor the United States can exercise, or will aspire
to exercise, any predominant rule in these regions."

nism, now when Germany was invading Russia, trampling
down and subjugating its people, any nation that would resist
and fight Hitler was Britain's ally.

Stalin, till the last moment, hoped against hope (and against
all evidence) that Hitler would not attack him. True to his suspicious nature, he also believed that Churchill's warnings to
him must be dismissed (and not only publicly); he believed
that it was Churchill's and Britain's interest to see the German
colossus turn eastward and get into a war with Russia, whence
he could not expect much, if anything, from Churchill. In sum,
he knew that Hitler's invasion of Russia was welcome to
Churchill, which of course it was; but he also misestimated
Churchill's motives, attributing to them, at least from time to
time, a cynical wish to goad the Germans or at least to help
bring about a German-Russian war. Stalin's misunderstandings marked much of their relationship during the war. But
there was also more than that. Churchill grew to like Stalin,
or at least some of his qualities; and Stalin grew to respect
Churchill, or at least to believe what he was saying.

In Churchill's case there were two elements at work in this
now evolving relationship. One was his relief, at times rising
to admiration, in seeing Stalin as a great national leader in
war; the other was Churchill's enduring contempt for Communism. But for several months after June 1941 there was not
much reason for Churchill to raise his estimation of Stalin.
From June to December 1941 Churchill's main concern was to
see America edging closer and closer to war, and to help keep
Russia fighting. There was a crisis in September and October
1941 which historians of the Second World War may not have

examined closely enough. In early September, Stalin sent a
message to Churchill, including ominous words: "The Soviet
Union is in a position of mortal peril" — which it was, with the
Germans racing ahead in Russia, corralling millions of Russian prisoners. In that abject message* Stalin showed his igno-
rance: he asked for a British invasion of Western Europe, and
the deployment of twenty-five or thirty British divisions to
Russia itself, through Persia or Archangel.† Churchill told him
that this was impossible. Meanwhile, British war production
was strained to its limits (and at a very difficult time), sending
as many tanks and airplanes to Russia as was possible. Britain
and Russia had already signed a kind of alliance; and they sub-
dued and occupied Persia jointly in a matter of days. Churchill
was not a secretive statesman: but we do not quite know what
he thought of Stalin in September and October 1941, when a
decisive German victory in Russia seemed indeed possible.‡
In any event — Churchill's composure during this, now largely

* It may be interesting that this phrase was slightly altered in the
Soviet edition of the Stalin-Churchill correspondence. ("This has re-
sulted in a lessening of our defense capacity and has confronted the
Soviet Union with mortal danger.")

† Shades of Lenin! It is a pity that it did not come about. What a
book Evelyn Waugh could have written about the adventures of the
Royal Fusiliers in the Ukraine. (Possible titles: *The Red Miss Chief; Com-
rades in Arms; Kommissarovka Revisited*.") I wrote some of this a quarter-
century ago; cf. *The Last European War, 1939–1941*, New York, 1976,
rpt. 2001, p. 149.

‡ It is at least interesting that in early September Churchill sent Lord
Beaverbrook to interview Rudolf Hess in secret. See also *The Last European War*, p. 149, note 22.

forgotten, period of crisis was remarkable. Then came the turning point of the entire war, in December 1941. The Russians stopped and turned back the German advance before Moscow at the very moment when half a globe away, the Japanese attack on Pearl Harbor propelled the United States into the war.

Churchill was relieved. He now knew that the Japanese (and Hitler) were doomed. He also realized that Russia had come through the worst, with Stalin as her great leader, indeed, a statesman to boot. The week before Pearl Harbor and the Moscow turn Churchill had to accede to Stalin's repeated requests to declare war on Finland, Hungary, Rumania (he minded the first much more than the last), governments that had gone to war against Russia on Hitler's side. The week after Pearl Harbor he sent Anthony Eden to Moscow, where Stalin demanded that Britain recognize what Russia wanted after the war: at least a restoration of its 1941 boundaries, including incorporation of the Baltic states and of eastern Poland. Churchill was able to evade such a formal commitment, but barely. Also, more and more instances of Russian brutalities and ambitions were beginning to appear, their evidences mostly experienced and reported by Poles. There was a meeting between Churchill and the Polish Prime Minister in exile, Gen. Wladyslaw Sikorski, in March 1942, recounted by the latter. Churchill admitted "that his own assessment of Russia did not differ much" from that of his Polish friend. "However, he underlined the reasons which made it necessary" to make certain agreements with Russia. "She was the only country that had fought against the Germans with success. She had destroyed millions of German soldiers and at present the aim of the war seemed not so much victory, as the death or survival of our allied nations. Should Russia come to an agreement with the Reich, all would be lost. It must not happen. If Russia was victorious she would decide on her frontiers without consulting Great Britain; should she lose the war, the agreement would lose all its importance."* There is every reason to believe that this daunting and somber assessment was more than a realistic reminder to a minor, and occasionally troubling, ally. It represented Churchill's deepest thoughts about the war. For by March 1942 much of the relief of three months before had paled, if not vanished altogether. The turning around near Moscow went only so far. Where Napoleon had failed, Hitler succeeded. The German armies lived through the winter in Russia, getting ready to advance again. The Japanese advanced, too, in leaps and bounds. Singapore had surrendered. In the Atlantic, American and British ships were sunk by Germany's submarines. From June to December 1941 Stalin had been dependent on Churchill. Now Churchill was becoming dependent on Stalin.

There were a few instances during the war when Churchill was anxious about the excessive admiration for Russia and about the rise of Communist influences in Britain; yet he attributed not much importance to that. Unlike to people on the Left (and of course unlike German and pro-German propaganda), Communism and Russia, Communists and Stalin were

*Documents of Polish-Soviet Relations, 1939–1945, London, 1961, 1: 297–298.

matters not at all identical to his mind. We can see this later in the war, when he used the dismissive word *Trotskyist* to categorize foreign Communist revolutionaries who seemed to act independent of Stalin. He was not altogether wrong. For example, most Communists in the United States, often Jewish, though committed Stalinists, were essentially Trotsky-like in their beliefs in International Communism or the class struggle or whatnot: but that is another story. Our main story is Churchill's relationship to Stalin, and their mutual dependence, in the balance of which Stalin weighed more heavily than Churchill, certainly in 1942. And so Churchill flew across half the world to meet him.

I come now to their meetings in Moscow, to the two "summits" of August 1942 and October 1944, which were crucial for their relationship. In 1942 they learned to know each other; in 1944 they divided Eastern Europe between themselves. These summits were at least as important as, if not more important than, the tripartite summits in Teheran (1943), Yalta (1945) and Potsdam (1945), the first two including Roosevelt, the third Truman (not to speak of Churchill's half-dozen meetings with Roosevelt from 1941 to 1944). In August 1942 Churchill flew across Africa and Asia to Moscow. Not merely to establish a personal relationship; he had plenty of explaining to do. Again the Germans were crashing through southern Russia, entering the Caucasus; the Americans were struggling with the Japanese in the far southwestern reaches of the Pacific; Rommel was pushing the British back into Egypt; scores of British vessels were sent to the bottom of the Atlantic and Arctic seas; all the British could and would do was bomb certain German cities at night. Worse: Churchill had to tell Stalin what the latter had already expected: that there would be no Second Front in Western Europe in 1942. (Churchill and his generals had been able to dissuade Roosevelt and Marshall from that — rightly, for it would have been a disaster.) Stalin spoke roughly. But Churchill gave as good as he got. That impressed Stalin. He often appreciated the courage and the spirit of those (there were not many) who stood up to him. Churchill, at his turn, was impressed by Stalin, too: by his rough readiness; by his qualities of a national chieftain but also those of a father; by Stalin's invocation of God, at least on one occasion. Churchill was also relieved, and impressed, by Stalin's reaction to the only considerable good news he had brought: that of the planned American-British invasion of French North Africa in November. Stalin was not excessively grateful: but he seemed to instantly comprehend what that meant for the war.

After this first summit in Moscow, Churchill (we do not know exactly when for the first time) would occasionally say to his circle: "I like this man." But there was worse to follow. After Stalingrad the Russian beast got the bit in its teeth. Stalin was demanding: Churchill and Roosevelt had to give more and more consideration to him. In 1943 their relations turned worse than before. Stalin realized that there would be no Second Front even in that year. Some of his gestures (for instance, his withdrawal of his well-known ambassadors from London and Washington) were ominous. He thought, and said, that the British were simply not doing enough to carry their full weight in this war. There was real trouble swirling about Poland. Churchill thought that this was not the time to confront

Stalin about his postwar purposes. He admired how the Russians fought. It was not his idea to present Stalin — at Teheran — with the "Sword of Stalingrad": but it was in accord with his romantic sentiments. "In accord": but was he carried away by his liking for Stalin? No — there was a dual tendency in his mind about Stalin and the Russians, a duality that was not oscillating but nearly always constant. There are many evidences for this. In October 1943 Gen. Henry Pownall recorded that Churchill "thoroughly disliked the Russians and their ways and is under no illusions about them. They are doing what they are doing (and very well indeed) to save their own skins. Their future policy will be entirely to suit themselves and nobody else will count. All the more necessary, of course, to keep along with the U.S."* At another time Churchill said that the Soviets were like crocodiles, one never knew when to pat their heads or hit them.

Then came the tripartite summit at Teheran. There Churchill lost his once dominant position, and he knew it: he had slipped behind Roosevelt and Stalin. His disappointment (carefully hidden, even in his War Memoirs) was with Roosevelt rather than with Stalin: for the American president made a show of distancing himself from Churchill, trying to impress Stalin that he, Roosevelt, was at least as close to him (if not closer) as he was to the Britisher. Many things were discussed and decided at Teheran. Stalin was relieved to know that the full invasion of Western Europe would finally come late next

*Henry Pownall, Chief of Staff: The Diaries of Lieutenant General Sir Henry Pownall, 1940–1944, Brian Bond, ed., London, 1974, 2: 109–110.

spring, though he was still suspicious that Churchill would wish to delay or change that. But by that time Stalin knew, too, that to keep his good relations with the United States was even more important than his relations with Britain.

Churchill knew that. But he knew, too, that — as far as Europe was concerned — his relations with Russia were as important as were his relations with the United States. Moreover, because of the advancing geography of the war, they were becoming imminent: questions and problems and plans that could not be for long postponed. They involved, first and foremost, the prospective division of Europe. I wrote earlier of the — at first sight, brutally consistent — Churchillian (and British) realization that half of Europe was better than none; that if the alternative to Germany ruling Europe was Russia ruling Eastern Europe, so be it. This is plainly put, but there was now more to that. Looking further ahead, Churchill was beginning to be concerned with two weighty matters. Germany's domination of Europe, God willing and D day succeeding, was coming to its end. That happening, the liberation of Western Europe was a foregone conclusion. But what about the rest of Europe then? Would Germany be divided? Churchill thought that perhaps for the better, yes, along historical lines: but he was not sure what Stalin and Roosevelt had in mind about Germany, and he did not push that problem forward, not even at Yalta. But east and southeast of Germany the question of Eastern Europe, unlike the question of Germany, was becoming imminent. Churchill and Stalin knew that; Roosevelt did not — for many reasons, including the American habit not to think of unpleasant future things, and including also Roosevelt's habit of procrastination, especially in 1944, allied with his wish to avoid any kind of trouble with Stalin.

We come now to the problems of Poland and of Eastern Europe, in some ways similar, in others different. There was, to begin with, a moral commitment to Poland that Churchill would not dismiss, for reasons deeper than politic. It was because of Hitler's invasion of Poland that Britain had declared war on Germany. But Britain's guarantee to and its alliance with Poland in 1939 helped Poland not at all. At the same time the Poles fought with exceptional bravery. Nearly one hundred thousand of them made their way to Britain, many of them soldiers and airmen of outstanding qualities. They fought in the air, on the seas, and on three continents, on the British side. There existed a British obligation to them, no matter how difficult to fulfill. That was not something that Churchill would consider only for internal political reasons (unlike Roosevelt, who startled Stalin by telling him that he needed Polish-American votes in certain precincts in important states). But then there was geography. It was through Poland that the Germans massed and then marched into Russia; and it would be through Poland that the Russians would march into Germany. It was at least conceivable that in some places of southeastern Europe, British or Anglo-American forces could appear near or at the end of the war; but in northeastern Europe, and particularly Poland, this was impossible. So Churchill's hands were bound, even when his mind was not.

He could not ignore, let alone defy, what Stalin wanted from Poland. Stalin wanted two things: his 1941 frontiers, and next to them a subservient Poland. In the end he got both, though

Churchill fought hard about the second. The first was the easier problem — for him, though not for the Poles. The Soviet
Union's western frontier in 1941 (which it reached in 1939 by
the pact with Hitler) ran, by and large, along the so-called Curzon Line of 1920 (proposed by the British and the French governments during the Soviet-Polish war in 1920 but which after
the defeat of the Red Army in that war was dropped; in the
Treaty of Riga, 1921, the Polish-Russian frontier was set more
than one hundred miles farther east). From the beginning
Churchill thought that he should not and could not deny this
primary Russian demand. Also, among other matters, this portion of eastern Poland was inhabited by all kinds of people,
the majority of whom were not Poles. On the other hand, a
Polish acceptance of the Curzon Line would amount to a loss
of more than two-fifths of prewar Polish land. The exiled Polish government in London — unlike many other exile governments, not a shadow regime but one with considerable prestige and a substantial army, would not assent to that.

Churchill's idea was to balance the geographic concession
against a political one: to grant Stalin the Curzon Line, in exchange for his acceptance of an independent Poland, deter-
minedly friendly to Russia, but with a government not domi-
nated by Moscow's chosen people, subservient Communists.
He must not be criticized for having failed in this. The Polish
government in London would not accept the Curzon Line till
the very end — even though Churchill, with Stalin's consent,
proposed a very sizable compensation for Poland, with large
territories to be acquired from Germany. Roosevelt and the
Americans gave Churchill little or no support. More impor-

tant: by 1944 Stalin, whose armies had begun to advance across
Poland, knew that he would get both the Curzon Line and
a satellite government in Warsaw, ruled by mostly Moscow-
trained Communists. That the fate of Poland was not a minor
concern for Churchill is obvious from the condition that, upon
his insistence, Poland took up most of the time at Yalta as well
as during his Moscow conference with Stalin in October 1944.
During that conference he spoke rudely and at times brutally
to the democratic Polish representatives who were still un-
willing and unable to accept the Curzon Line; Churchill said
that he would not allow them to threaten his wartime alliance
with Stalin; he excoriated them for their stubbornness and
unrealism, for missing (so he told them) their last and only
chance to secure a decent and free Poland after the war. Stalin, after all, had allowed some of the Poles from London to
come to Moscow, while Churchill showed nothing but contempt for the Communist or pro-Communist Poles whom Stalin had produced as the leaders of his Poland. (Churchill was
impressed — though not assuaged — to see that Stalin, too,
did not think much of the latter. With something like a twin-
kle in his eye, Stalin signaled his satisfaction to Churchill to
the effect: "See how my puppets obey . . .")

This conference in Moscow, lasting almost ten days, offers
many clues to the Churchill-Stalin relationship. Churchill saw
it as a success, reporting thus to London both during and after
it. Perhaps he was overly sanguine; perhaps he overestimated
what he saw as evidences of Stalin's realism — and consequently of their relationship, of their reciprocal, if not mutual,
esteem. He has been criticized for his behavior in Moscow. Yet

he tried, and at least in part succeeded, to save what he could: to save from Stalin's clutch as much of Europe as he then could, at a time when he, Churchill, had no trumps in his hand. There was to be no Anglo-American military presence in Eastern Europe. He had failed to impress the Americans. Meanwhile, the Russians had overrun Rumania and Bulgaria, moved into Yugoslavia, and were grinding their way across Hungary. Months before that Churchill posed a, perhaps rhetorical, question to Anthony Eden: are we willing to acquiesce in the Communization of the Balkans and, perhaps, of Italy? In June he suggested a temporary division of labor to the Russians (and also to Roosevelt), amounting, in essence, that a line of a division of responsibilities should be drawn, with Rumania and Bulgaria going to the Russians. But there was no definite American agreement to this, as indeed not in other matters. So Churchill, upon arriving in Moscow, sat down across the table from Stalin and proposed his Percentages Agreement.

Every so often the Percentages Agreement is brought out as evidence of Churchill's cynicism, as an indication of the breezy way with which this haughty old aristocrat would dispose of the fate of entire nations. This criticism is misplaced. In a way its opposite was true. There is not the slightest indication that anyone in the British government (including Eden), any important official in the Foreign Office, any influential British public personage, any press lord had tried to remind Churchill that something had to be done to ascertain and establish the limits of a total Soviet control of southeastern Europe, including Hungary. The idea, and the concern, was Churchill's own. It was the first, and pressing, matter on his agenda. At the very first moment of his first meeting with Stalin he said that they must discuss Poland, and then he immediately went on. The story is well known. No one described it as directly and graphically as did Churchill himself. He pushed a half-sheet of paper across the table, on which he had written these percentages: "Roumania: Russia 90%. Greece: Great Britain (in accord with USA) 90%. Yugoslavia: 50–50. Hungary: 50–50. Bulgaria: Russia 75%." Stalin took his customary blue pencil and made a big check mark on the paper. All right! "After this there was a long silence. The pencilled paper lay in the centre of the table. At length I said: 'Might it not be thought rather cynical if it seemed we had disposed of these issues, so fateful to millions of people, in such an offhand way?' Let us burn the paper. 'No, you keep it, said Stalin.' "* Churchill was impressed. This was to be a successful conference; and Stalin could be relied upon.

It was not quite that; and yet Churchill was not entirely wrong. It was not quite that: we have already seen that Churchill made hardly a dent in Stalin's determination of what to do about Poland. Also, a day or so after that momentous agreement, Stalin told Molotov to haggle with Eden over some of its details. Molotov was a harder haggler than Eden; he redrew some of the percentages (especially in the case of Hungary) in Russia's favor, and Churchill let that stand — perhaps also because he had come down with a severe case of the flu. Yet his esteem for Stalin was stronger than ever before; at least

* Churchill's own account, *Triumph and Tragedy*, Boston, 1953, pp. 227–228.

on one occasion he referred to Stalin as "a great and good man." At least in one important instance Stalin did keep his word. Churchill had proposed 90 percent, near-absolute, British predominance in Greece; Stalin accepted that without a murmur. This was important, because Churchill had much to worry about in Greece, where civil war was in the offing, because a Communist partisan army was growing almost everywhere, trying to defeat and eliminate the royalist and liberal Greek resistance forces — this despite the first arrival of a few British troops in Athens during the very time of the Moscow conference. Yet the Percentages Agreement saved Greece* — Churchill's principal purpose. Five weeks later a Communist insurrection seemed to overwhelm Athens. Churchill sent a considerable British force from Italy to resist and suppress it. In darkest December he abandoned his prospect of a family Christmas and flew to Greece to hammer out an interim political solution. He had incurred sharp, and often violent, criticism from the Americans, including the State Department and the press; but not a single bad word or act from Stalin. (The Russian member of the Allied Control Commission in Athens told the, momentarily triumphant, Communists that he had nothing to do with them.) Once or twice Churchill called the Greek Communists "Trotskyists" — meaning that they were not like Stalin.

---

*It could not save Hungary, even though Churchill insisted several times (mostly to the Americans) during the next few months that Hungary was not a Balkan but a Central European state, and that (contrary to one of Stalin's remarks) Hungary did not border on Russia.

He saw Stalin as a traditional Russian ruler — a statesman, a Red Tsar. Attacking Churchill after the war, Evelyn Waugh wrote that Churchill had thought Stalin was just an old Tsar writ large, "a frightful mistake." But of course Stalin *was* a Tsar writ large: only not that shuffling, bumbling, kindly Nicholas II type, with his spade beard, resembling that of George V of England, but a monstrous Tsar writ large, a new Ivan the Terrible. What Churchill also understood was that geography and territory mattered, not ideology; where the Russian armies and where the Anglo-American armies would stand at the end of the war, and that the way to deal with Stalin was therefore on a quid pro quo basis — this is yours, this is ours. Stalin understood matters in much of the same way. (Roosevelt and the Americans did not, except when and where they were compelled to do so by circumstances.)

At the Yalta Conference in February 1945 Churchill was still a principal figure, but his power and his influence were less than those of Roosevelt and Stalin. Poland was still a principal and long-debated subject at Yalta, but Stalin gave little or nothing. Churchill's personal relations with him were still excellent. They toasted each other, perhaps excessively. At Yalta, Stalin went almost so far as to congratulate Churchill for having laid down the law in Greece; Churchill told the British representatives in Rumania that they must understand the great limitations of Britain's interests there. But very soon after Yalta — notwithstanding the Percentages Agreement — Churchill recognized that "The Declaration of Liberated Europe," a generalized statement drafted and signed at Yalta, mainly to please President Roosevelt, promising "democracy" everywhere in Europe, was seen by Stalin to mean that what *his* armies had "liberated" belonged to him. It was thus imperative that the Anglo-American armies meet the Russians as far east as was possible. For some time Churchill had hoped and occasionally planned for a British force to arrive in Vienna; his plans were scotched by the Americans. But in late March a new situation was developing. Across Germany the Anglo-American armies were racing forward faster than the Russians. If not Vienna, they might reach Prague or perhaps even Berlin ahead of the Russians. The Americans would have nothing of that. The Allied Supreme Commander General Eisenhower took it upon himself to inform Stalin (without informing Churchill beforehand) that the Allied armies would not advance in that direction.

Churchill's problems with the Americans, with Roosevelt and his circle (the President was dying), were now as difficult as were his problems with Stalin. He took excessive care not to make this public at the time, or even seven years later, when he dictated the pertinent volume of his War Memoirs. (He did that to please Eisenhower, the incoming President and his former wartime comrade — we shall see in a succeeding chapter, to no avail.) Stalin knew something about the differences between Churchill and the Americans. On occasion he was even able to play them against each other, at least a little. But by March 1945 his main concern was different: where would his armies meet the Anglo-Americans within Germany? He was incensed to learn that since early February, Allen Dulles, a secret American representative in Switzerland, had been negotiating with a German SS general about the eventual sur-

render of the German army in Italy to the Anglo-Americans.
(Stalin was not altogether wrong: those parleys were but another German attempt to drive a wedge between the Anglo-
Americans and the Russians. Nor were they undertaken behind Hitler's back or against his will.) Stalin was even more
concerned with the easy and rapid surrender of German cities
and troops to the Allies in western Germany, while Germans
fought bitterly and hard for every village in Silesia or Prussia
or even in Czech Bohemia. Roosevelt did not quite know how
to respond to Stalin's angry charges: but it was no longer he
who drafted his answers to Stalin, the tones of which were at
times contradictory. On 12 April he died. Had he much earlier
shown Stalin (and the world) that he and Churchill were in
unison about important matters, Churchill's position as the
principal statesman of the West at the end of the war would
have been immeasurably stronger. But this was not to be: and,
so far as Europe went, Churchill did not have his way. The
Russians occupied Vienna, Berlin, Prague. A few days before
Hitler killed himself, Heinrich Himmler offered the uncondi-
tional surrender of the Third Reich to the Western Allies.
Churchill rejected this: surrender must involve all of the Allies, including the Soviet Union. Stalin's reaction was, for
once, fulsome. "Knowing you, I had no doubt that you would
act in this way." For once Churchill's vanity had the better of
him: he was very much cheered by Stalin's words.

But such elation was fleeting. All through those weeks of
victories and of the sinking of Hitler's Third Reich, Churchill's
mood was somber — perhaps more somber than at any time
since May 1940. His wife went on a tour of Russia and was

received with much cordiality and goodwill. Yet passages of his letters to her are telling. (On 2 April: "At the moment you are the one bright spot in Anglo-Russian relations." On 8 April: "Well you know how great our difficulties are about Poland, Rumania, and this other row about alleged negotiations. I intend still to persevere, but it is very difficult." On 5 May: "I need scarcely tell you that beneath these triumphs lie poisonous politics and deadly international rivalries."* He realized, better than anyone else, what Stalin's interpretation of the Yalta declarations meant: among them the absence of any sign, or hope, that Stalin would permit anything like a more or less free and democratic government in Poland. In his V-E speeches Churchill warned the British people of more trials and challenges ahead. He went so far as to instruct Montgomery and other British commanders in Germany to collect German arms, holding them in reserve for an eventual confrontation with Russians advancing farther westward, beyond the occupation zones allotted to them. Among other matters, he wanted to make sure that the British army would meet the Russians east of the entry to the Danish peninsula. And there was, he thought, one important trump card left: the fact that in central Germany the advancing Anglo-American armies had met the Russians well east of the previously agreed zonal borders of occupation. Perhaps — perhaps — their withdrawal could be made contingent on Russian concessions, again principally about Poland.

---

*Mary Soames, ed., *Speaking for Themselves: The Personal Letters of Winston and Clementine Churchill,* London, 1998, pp. 522, 530.

But this was not to happen. There was a new American president now, Harry Truman, who soon demonstrated his bravery and strength of mind, standing up to Stalin, seeing – almost – eye to eye with Churchill; but not yet. During the fatal last months of the war – indeed, through most of the Zero Year, 1945 – the American government, the military, the Department of State, the press cheered on the Russians with very few exceptions. "They are ringing the bells," Walpole said about his critics two hundred years before. "Soon they will be wringing their hands." So it was with the Americans in 1945. At the last summit of the war, at Potsdam in July, nothing much of importance was discussed, besides a clouded acceptance of the status quo in Europe and in Germany. Now Churchill was worn and tired. His energy had weakened, his powers of concentration also; his attention to details, including important ones, was lagging, he did not do his homework before and during Potsdam – all this was noticed by his entourage. Stalin did not believe that Churchill would not be returned to office by his people in the July 1945 British election; Churchill could hardly believe that either. Yet so it happened.

We now come to the last phase of this extraordinary relationship with Stalin, marked by Churchill's sonorous warnings against Russia, and by the beginning of the cold war. He was no longer Prime Minister. But he was watching the evolution of events. He took some comfort from seeing how President Truman and the American government were, cautiously and gradually, changing their views about Stalin and Russia. Yet there was a difference between his and their perspectives. The Americans were increasingly worried about Communism, about the prospect of Stalin's influence and power extending into Western Europe, to Italy or France. Churchill was concerned with the growing rigidification of the division of Europe, with Stalin's increasing imposition of his total control over Eastern Europe and what that meant. Subsequently Churchill rose to President Truman's invitation, and made his famous Iron Curtain speech in Fulton, Missouri, March 1946. It soon became one of his most celebrated and historic speeches. Yet at the time the American reaction to it was mixed: even Truman thought that he must distance himself from it, at least a little; his confidant and later Secretary of State Dean Acheson disavowed it altogether. No matter: soon it was apparent that Churchill was right. Halifax, still British ambassador to Washington, advised Churchill to smooth things over, perhaps even go to Moscow to explain things to Stalin. No, Churchill said, that would be cringing, like apologizing to Hitler, say, in 1938.

Did this mean that Churchill had changed his mind about Stalin entirely? Yes and no — more accurately: no, rather than yes. He saw Stalin as a Russian tyrant, concerned with securing fast his acquired domains in Eastern Europe, while the Americans saw him as the head of World Communism, bent on increasing his domains further and further in Europe. Churchill thought that fears were often the sources of Stalin's brutal aggressiveness. They fear our friendship as much, if not more, than our enmity, Churchill would occasionally say. In 1951 he became Prime Minister again. The cold war was at its peak; there was a war fought in Korea; the Russians had their own atom bomb; there were many troubles elsewhere. Yet even before Stalin died Churchill saw some signs of change. We saw that on the last day of 1952 he said to Jock Colville that in about three decades Communism would disappear from Eastern Europe. Nine weeks later Stalin died. Churchill was convinced that the time had come to renegotiate some of the conditions of the cold war, including the conditions of a divided Europe, with the new, uneasy and unsure rulers of the Soviet Union. But this, too, was not to be.

Summing up: was Churchill wrong in his assessment — and in his treatment — of Stalin? His romantic temperament and his sentimental rhetoric did carry him too far, on occasion. But essentially he was not wrong. He kept that strange and difficult wartime alliance going, which was not easy, since Stalin's loyalty to his allies was not a foregone conclusion, not to speak of Hitler's intention to split the Allies or at least cause serious trouble between them. And about Eastern Europe: in 1944 Churchill did save Greece; and — unlike in 1815, after another world war, when another Russian Tsar did not allow a Polish state to exist — in 1945 there was a Polish state, though subservient to Moscow. Its existence and — more important — the gradual growth of Polish independence thereafter — were greatly due to the wartime bravery and to the resolution of Poles themselves: but, to a small extent at least, also to Winston Churchill.

3

Churchill and Roosevelt

A correspondence between two statesmen may conceal as much as it reveals. Their letters often suggest, rather than represent, the relationship of the writers. The three volumes of *Churchill and Roosevelt: The Complete Correspondence* (1984), edited by Warren F. Kimball, are an exception. They are the most nearly complete record of what may be the most voluminous correspondence that has ever been conducted between the leaders of two great nations — all of it through five years of a world war in which Churchill and Roosevelt were two of the four principal figures. Not only for the English-speaking peoples but for the history of the world, the relationship of Churchill and Roosevelt was and continues to be at least as interesting as the relationship of either of them with their difficult and distant ally Stalin. The Churchill-Roosevelt correspondence is not a contemplative one. It is a correspondence dealing with actions, decisions, dangers, and prospects: the record of two captains* speaking to each other in the midst of

---

*Captains, yes; but in 1942 Churchill at least on occasion (and jokingly) would refer to himself as "Roosevelt's lieutenant."

the greatest storm that had beset Western civilization. Before the Second World War began, Churchill and Roosevelt had sent a few distant messages to each other. Before the war ended, Roosevelt had died. But during the war — more precisely, between 11 September 1939 and 11 April 1945 — they exchanged nearly two thousand letters and telegrams, of which Churchill wrote 1,161 and Roosevelt 788. Some of these were printed, at least in part, in Churchill's grand compound of history and memoir, *The Second World War,* composed only a few years later. There have been other collections and editions of the Churchill-Roosevelt correspondence since that time, but with Kimball's exhaustive compilation we have something like a near-complete picture: a huge packet of letters and messages which is a monument of the now passing civilization of the past five centuries — no less a monument than, say, the Colosseum in the age of Rome or the city of Paris in the Modern Age.

One reason for such a, seemingly extreme, statement is that no remotely similar correspondence between two great statesmen has occurred since; and the likelihood of its occurring now is about equal to the likelihood of someone's writing a symphony in the manner of Schubert. For many reasons, including the danger of the Germans' listening to and unscrambling telephonic communications, most of Churchill's and Roosevelt's exchanges were made in writing. Since then all kinds of changes, cultural as well as technological, have reduced the necessity and the practice of such written communications between statesmen. Instead of the telephone, Churchill strenuously preferred the written word. This was not always to his advantage. Like many of the great masters of language, he was inclined to trust the influence of his words unduly. He would dictate a message, putting his best efforts into phrasing his propositions clearly, strongly, including every possible argument and detail to sustain his thesis. Once he had expended his energy, care, and precision on full statement of his propositions, a diminution of his resolution would sometimes follow — especially during the two last years of the war, when his physical strength and his capacity for concentration were weakening. From the beginning to the end of the war Churchill drafted his letters and messages himself. Roosevelt, as the war went on, and as his health and energy began to fail, relied on the drafts of others (we know the names of some of the drafters). This made a difference, but, except for a few cases, probably not a decisive one.

Sometime in the fall of 1938 — after Munich and more than three years before Pearl Harbor — Roosevelt began to offer his support, cautiously, privately, and secretly, to a few persons in England and France who were opposed to a further appeasement of Hitler. Foremost among these men was Churchill. There was no written communication between the two men during the year before the war broke out. Yet Roosevelt knew, like everyone else, that it was because of Churchill's record of warnings against Hitler that Chamberlain was compelled to invite Churchill into his War Cabinet as the First Lord of the Admiralty; and a few days later Roosevelt sent his first letter to Churchill, who responded eagerly to this friendly and important signal from the New World. He told Chamberlain and his Foreign Secretary Halifax about this special correspondence. They fully approved of it. Eight months later Churchill became Prime Minister. He knew that somehow, somewhere, at some time, the United States would have to come into the war on the side of Britain. Roosevelt knew it, too, though he would fain not admit it to the American people. Churchill knew that Roosevelt knew. Before the tremendous importance of this meeting of minds their eventual misunderstandings and disagreements pale. Without Roosevelt's support, the British would have had to make peace with Hitler, accepting Germany's domination of Europe. I emphasize Europe, not the Far East, because this, too, was an essential element in Churchill's and Roosevelt's meeting of minds. Well before Pearl Harbor, Roosevelt realized that a war against Germany must have priority over an eventual war against Japan; a defeat of the second would follow the defeat of the first. This American decision was not inevitable: there were many domestic and military pressures to the contrary. That Roosevelt saw eye to eye with Churchill on this was of the utmost importance.

Both Churchill and Roosevelt were Naval Persons ("Former Naval Person" was the code name that Churchill used in his correspondence with Roosevelt during most of the war). But Roosevelt had an exaggerated confidence in the importance of naval power, which after four centuries was beginning to lessen. At the time of the French collapse, Roosevelt tried to console the French Prime Minister: naval power was still the key to war and history, he wrote. In 1941 he wrote to Churchill that "in the last analysis the Naval control of the Indian Ocean and the Atlantic Ocean will in time win the war." Yet in the

Second World War a motorized land army could move faster than a navy. The war had to be won on the continent of Europe. It would end in the middle of Germany, in the ruins of Berlin. A few days after Churchill had become Prime Minister, when Western Europe was falling before Hitler's blows, he recognized what Roosevelt was thinking: if worst came to worst, the British fleet could sail away to the New World and join the American navy to secure the western Atlantic. Churchill wrote Roosevelt that while *he* would never surrender, the American President should recognize that, with Hitler winning, and without the prospect of American help, a British government might follow whose single card in an eventual armistice with Hitler would be the existence of an intact British fleet. Certain American historians, including Kimball, have seen Churchill's warning as a sly attempt to keep his options open. No: at that moment Churchill was a supreme realist, forced to remind Roosevelt of the bleakest of all possibilities. After a while this misunderstanding between them melted away. Because of Hitler's reluctance to risk an invasion of Britain, and because of a greater assurance of American help, Churchill's leadership became secure and the prospect of a Britain forced to seek an armistice with Hitler disappeared. By November 1940 the Battle of Britain, at least in the air, had been won, and Franklin Roosevelt had been elected President for an unprecedented third term.

A few days after that election Churchill composed a letter to Roosevelt. (He wrote two long drafts before the final version.) Germany, he wrote, "reached the maximum industrial effort by the end of 1939." He was wrong. The German economy would accomplish miracles during the war, reaching its maximum effort four years later, in spite of the hundreds of thousands of bombs cast on Germany by overwhelming Anglo-American air power. Churchill wrote that he was not asking for "a large American Expeditionary Army." Whether he really meant that in 1940 we cannot tell; probably not. He also looked ahead to a time when the two English-speaking democracies would govern the destinies of most of the world — a vision that he had espoused early in his life, and that accompanied him till the end of his days. "If we win victory, we shall have to assume the major responsibility for a new world order," he wrote. "If, however, our two countries are to be associated in defending freedom, and still more in rebuilding the world after the war, neither of them should be placed in a position of being the suppliant client of the other." Yet this was exactly what happened: as the war went on, Churchill's Britain became more and more dependent on the wealth and power of Roosevelt's United States. Also — second in order, though not in importance — was a condition that neither Churchill nor Roosevelt could foresee in 1940: for all the wealth and the sea and air predominance of the Anglo-American forces, they would not be able to defeat the Third Reich by themselves, without the primitive might of Russia. It was Hitler's attack on Russia, mounted on the pretext and in the name of anti-Communism, that eventually led to the survival of Britain and to the global victory of the United States.

Churchill and Roosevelt learned this fast. It explains their forbearance toward Russian demands, including ones that were impossible to fulfill. It explains even more their respect for and trust in Stalin, expressed in the — in retrospect, strangely flowery — language of their telegrams and toasts to him. But Churchill's and Roosevelt's views of Stalin and Russia diverged. That Russia would share the spoils of victory over Germany in Europe was inevitable. What was not inevitable was the extent — extent, rather than nature — of the Russian dominion over most of Eastern and parts of Central Europe: in sum, the origins of the cold war. In his introduction Kimball writes that Churchill "had simply replaced the evil of Nazi Germany with the evil of the Soviet Union. Regardless of whether he was right about the Soviets, Churchill failed to acknowledge that the inevitable price of victory is the collapse of wartime alliances, no matter how strong the personal bonds." This is too simple. The de facto Anglo-American alliance survived the war. More important: Churchill's view of the Soviets and his proposals for dealing with them were more realistic than Roosevelt's. Their correspondence provides ample evidence of this.

There were many elements in Roosevelt's wish to dissociate himself from Churchill as the war drew on. Roosevelt trusted in his own charm: he believed, and said, that he could handle Stalin better than most people, including Churchill. He wanted Stalin to join in the war against Japan. He wanted to avoid any American entanglement in the politics of Central and Eastern Europe. He thought that the American people would not stand for a protracted stay of American troops in Europe after the war. He thought that getting Stalin's Russia into the United Nations was a great prize. Some of these considerations may have been reasonable at the time; others were not. Underlying them were personal inclinations that proved to have been decisive. One was Roosevelt's habit of procrastinating, his unwillingness to confront certain problems — a practice that sometimes worked for him in domestic politics but that became more and more pronounced as he declined in strength and health.

Roosevelt's increasing wish to distance himself from Churchill during the last years of the war requires further explanation. For a long time their exceptional relationship prevailed. Their mutual affection may have reached its peak in 1942 — that is, after Churchill had become very much the junior partner in their alliance. They met first on warships off Newfoundland in August 1941, and again in Washington after Pearl Harbor. That second meeting took place under the shadow of disastrous British defeats, but somehow their personal friendship solidified then. Even the condition that neither Eleanor nor Elliott Roosevelt had much liked Churchill then made little difference. It was after all in 1942 that Roosevelt wrote Churchill, "It is fun to be in the same decade with you." And in 1942, and even for some part of 1943, Churchill could have his way. He succeeded in persuading Roosevelt and the American high military command that their proposed invasion of France in late 1942 would be a disaster. He succeeded in persuading them a year later that the Allied victory in North Africa should be followed by an invasion of Sicily and of the Italian mainland. Even Roosevelt's strictures on and proposals against British rule in India made not much difference: the President dropped the issue, without Churchill having to make much fuss about it. But then there came a change — gradually but definitely. By the time of the Teheran summit, the first one among the Big Three, the change had crystallized. Roosevelt tried his best — and, at times, his worst — to distance himself from Churchill; to indicate to Stalin that he had no special relationship with Churchill. And when, in 1944, Churchill pleaded with Roosevelt to exploit the campaign in Italy and move some of the Anglo-American forces in the direction of Vienna, to insist on the problem of Poland before it became too late, to settle something about the future of the Danubian states of Central Europe before the Russians occupied and possessed them, to make use of a situation when — finally, in the spring of 1945 — the Anglo-American armies were moving across Germany faster than the Russians, Roosevelt refused. Before Yalta, Churchill wrote to Roosevelt, "This may well be a fateful conference, coming at a moment when the great allies are so divided and the shadow of the war lengthens out before us. At the present time I think the end of this war may well prove to be more disappointing than was the last." Roosevelt did not see it this way. He refused to confer with Churchill before Yalta, save for a few hours in Malta Harbor. There Churchill wrote that it was "undesirable that more of . . . Europe than necessary should be occupied by the Russians." But Roosevelt did not want to discuss that.

By early April 1945 the problems posed by Russian behavior had become acute. There is a telegram, one of the very last, that Roosevelt sent to Churchill from Warm Springs in Georgia six days before he died. He wrote that he was "pleased with your very clear strong message to Stalin. . . . Our armies will in a very few days be in a position that will permit us to become 'tougher' than has heretofore appeared advantageous to the war effort." For many years this telegram has been cited by Roosevelt's defenders who — especially during the ugly years of the McCarthy period — wanted to prove that if Roosevelt had lived he would have turned to resist Communist aggressiveness as rapidly and as forcefully as his successor Harry Truman did. We now know that this was not so. The message was drafted by Admiral Leahy, one person on the President's staff who did not like the Russians. (He was also suspicious of the British.) There are even reasons to believe that Roosevelt, sick, had not read it at all.

Churchill insisted that his affection for the United States, his gratitude for the American alliance, his memory of Franklin Roosevelt were as strong as ever. With every reason: in 1940 and after he could not have prevailed long without Roosevelt's support. He never forgot that, and not merely for politic considerations. It is regrettable that many Americans — including the Roosevelts but especially the President's circle, and all kinds of historical writers since then — attributed to Churchill imperialist calculations and schemes of which Americans had to be suspicious. In reality, it was Churchill who, in his relationship with Roosevelt, was the more open, more emotional, more romantic, less reserved, and less suspicious one. But there were moments when his easy high spirits affected Roosevelt too. Of course Churchill was the better writer. (Once in a while a Roosevelt message ends with a flat Americanism: "Keep up the good work.")

Yet there is more to be said about the Churchill-Roosevelt relationship than what appears from the exceptional measure of their wartime correspondence. In this short chapter I shall merely attempt to sum up three issues. One is the question of additional evidence, and its purposeful falsifications. Another is the "revisionist" writing of certain historians. A third is my concluding attempt to suggest something about the personal relationship of these two statesmen — always keeping in mind that while a historian's mind may be furnished by his extensive knowledge of documentary evidence, as well as by his understanding of human nature, both his knowledge and his understanding remain necessarily incomplete.

Churchill and Roosevelt had many conversations that were unrecorded: private and telephone talks. At least two — possibly more — of their telephone conversations were captured by German intelligence. The German Ministry of Posts set up a radiotelephone listening station in western Holland, where technicians were able to break into the so-called "scrambler" radiotelephone circuit set up between London and the United States in late 1941, the security of which, though considerable, was not perfect (the British knew that). One significant Churchill-Roosevelt conversation, four days after the fall of Mussolini, on 29 July 1943, seems to have been recorded *in toto:* a summary of it was immediately transmitted to the German High Command as well as to Hitler. A reproduction of this summary exists in print; however, I have not been able to acquire a copy of the entire transcript, even though I made a number of such attempts in Germany and England. The reason for my interest in this was my suspicion — which then hardened into a conviction — that a printed and published version of this conversation is a falsification. It was printed in a curious volume containing alleged interviews and interrogations of Heinrich Müller, the head of the Gestapo, who (probably with the connivance of Allen Dulles) was brought secretly to the United States in 1948 and interrogated by American secret services, and who eventually died and was buried in secrecy in America. That is interesting enough, but its further examination does not fit within the province of this book. Relevant to it are some of the documents that Müller said he had brought with him, including the abovementioned Churchill-Roosevelt telephone exchange, reprinted in a volume* edited by "Gregory Douglas" (possibly a pseudonym). My careful reading of this document suggested from the beginning that it was a clever concoction. (One instance of my original suspicions: Churchill frequently calling Roosevelt "Franklin," contrary to his custom.) My doubts were subsequently proved by men and women who knew Churchill intimately, including a full and detailed confirmation by an Englishwoman, a telephone "censor," whose duty had been to listen in to these telephone exchanges, and who had the authority to interrupt them at critical moments when, for instance, matters of high security were being talked about, for the purpose of warning the conversants.

There exist other clever falsifications involving Hitler — in most cases attributing to him statements that are either contrary to accepted views, or others that suggest astonishing foresights or prophecies on his part. They are clever, because

*Gestapo Chief: The 1948 Interrogation of Heinrich Müller, Gregory Douglas, ed., San Jose, Calif., 1995, pp. 56–62.

they often give an impression of authenticity: they include elements introduced to elevate Hitler's posthumous reputation, often carefully crafted by knowledgeable people. When it comes to Churchill, the purposes and methods are similar, but in a negative direction: the "evidence" is intended to blacken his reputation (and, at least indirectly, to whiten Hitler's). This is both the purpose and the method of David Irving, "revisionist" *primus inter pares,* but someone who, at least by this time, has been discredited to the extent that we must not take him seriously. However — we must keep in mind that there is revisionism and revisionism: that history is revisionist by its very nature; that there is no such thing as orthodox history, incontestable history, unchanging, unchangeable history nailed down forever. The revision of history must not be the ephemeral monopoly of ideologues or opportunists who are ever ready to twist or doctor or falsify evidences of the past in order to exemplify certain ideas, and their own adjustments to them. I am writing this because a magisterial reconstruction, and interpretation, of the Churchill-Roosevelt relationship may still be due: and perhaps especially from the perspective of the twenty-first century. After all, that relationship was but part of a very large theme, which is the British-American alliance and special relationship during the twentieth century, something that still persists here and there: but something that is bound to become problematic, sooner or later, because of the other large question, which is — and will be — Britain's relationship to Europe.

Churchill was astonishingly right about Hitler. He was also right about Communism and Stalin. About the first he was able to translate his views into action. About the second — because of his constraints but also because of American unwillingness — only partly so. This had much to do with the difference that separated Churchill's view of history from Franklin Roosevelt's. That they agreed that the prime object of the war was the defeat of Hitler's Third Reich was a blessing. (Recall that many of Roosevelt's American opponents did not agree: they believed that Communism was a much greater danger than was National Socialism, and Russia greater than Germany.) But consider too that Roosevelt saw the United States in the middle: in the middle not only between these two potential opponents, Churchill's Britain and Stalin's Russia, but in the middle of the progressive evolution of history, the historic position of the United States being in the middle between old Tory England and the rough pioneer experiment of the Soviet Union. (One example, Roosevelt speaking in 1944: "The great Republics, American and Soviet, standing shoulder to shoulder, each the sentinel in its own hemisphere, will together guarantee the peace and order of the world.") Churchill's view of the Soviet Union was very different: it was that of a powerful but backward empire, with its history and structure and civilization and mentality well behind those of the Western world — in any event, unfitting in such a scheme of evolutionary progress as seen by Roosevelt (and by many Americans) during the war.

This, I fear, has been insufficiently treated — and understood — by at least two historians of the Churchill-Roosevelt relationship, Professors Warren F. Kimball (an American) and

John Charmley (an Englishman). Kimball's precise collection and reproduction of the three volumes of the Churchill-Roosevelt correspondence is commendable; but his commentaries are not. The volumes are compromised by Kimball's "headnotes," introducing many of the documents. These include many dozens of errors, but also misunderstandings and attributions of thoughts and inclinations to Churchill that are wrong. One example (there are a number of others) which I felt compelled to mention in *Five Days in London* is Kimball's commentary on Churchill's message to Roosevelt at the dramatic time of France collapsing, 14–15 June 1940. According to Kimball, Churchill, "distraught . . . found it necessary to warn Roosevelt that Great Britain could not be expected to fight on alone without any real hope of American military intervention. His threat that a pro-German government might replace his Ministry was the first and one of the very few times that Churchill ever strayed from his usual strategy of emphasizing Britain's willingness to fight to the bitter end." It was not said for the first time; it was not a threat but a warning of something that had to be kept in mind; it was not a "strategy"; and it did not represent Churchill "straying." Charmley has written a number of books critical of Churchill. An analysis of his historianship does not belong to this chapter, but we must consider one basic element in Charmley's argument, which is that Churchill's gravest mistake was his easy, and often thoughtless, abdication to the United States. Charmley recently wrote that in the Second World War "the British were fighting . . . to preserve the empire of Victoria and the values it represented and held dear."* Yet the British people and most of their leaders had relinquished their Victorian imperialist standards and ideals long before 1939. I shall in a later chapter briefly return to Charmley's description of the historian Churchill ("a mythologist of [great] capacity and skill"); here it may suffice to state that his attribution of American selfishness and extortionism during the war is unbalanced and exaggerated, as is his American colleague Kimball's disingenuous attribution of Churchill's calculating imperialism.

A few last remarks about Churchill and the United States, and then about him and Roosevelt. I wrote earlier that Churchill, moved by a number of reasons and impulses, believed in the supreme importance of an ever-closer relationship between these two great English-speaking peoples almost throughout his life. We must qualify this. There were exceptions. He did not think much of Woodrow Wilson, and he was often critical of Americans and their policies and ideas after the First World War. His decision to restore the gold standard for the pound had much to do with his wish to see the pound become restored to its old exchange rate with the dollar. He was also against a British naval parity with the Americans, from 1918 almost until 1935. In June 1927 he said: "It always seems

---

*John Charmley, "Churchill and the American Alliance," in *Churchill and the Twenty-First Century: A Conference Held at the Institute of Historical Research, University of London, 11–13 January 2001, Transactions of the Royal Historical Society*, series 6, vol. XI, London, 2001, p. 358.

to be assumed that it is our duty to humour the United States and minister to their vanity. They do nothing for us in return, but exact their last pound of flesh."* On one occasion he called Calvin Coolidge "a New England backwoodsman" who would sink and fade into an obscurity which he well deserved; on another occasion he called Herbert Hoover a son of a bitch. Nor did Churchill's relationship with Roosevelt begin easily. They had actually met once in 1919, when Roosevelt was Assistant Secretary of the navy; Roosevelt remembered this in 1940, while it seems that Churchill did not. The first remarks of Roosevelt upon the news of Churchill's premiership were not complimentary. Some of Roosevelt's people thought that Churchill was too old; that he was drinking too much; again others (like Mrs. Roosevelt) that he was reactionary and imperialist. Soon much of this faded away. Yet Mrs. Roosevelt remained suspicious of Churchill, and of his vision of world politics, for a long time. This is remarkable because, despite the problems with their marriage, Franklin Roosevelt was, at least to a minor extent, influenced by his wife's views of the world throughout the war. Roosevelt was also slightly jealous and dismissive of Churchill's mental vivacity and of his rhetorical capacity. At the same time Roosevelt's anticolonialist, that is, pro-Indian and pro-Chinese, advocacies and exhortations were not as deep-seated as some historians, in this case espe-

*Quoted by Phillips O'Brien in "Churchill and the U.S. Navy 1919–29," in *Winston Churchill: Studies in Statesmanship*, R. A. C. Parker, ed., London, 1995.

cially Kimball and Charmley, have taken them to have been.*
It was in relation to Russia and to postwar Europe that
Churchill's and Roosevelt's views diverged considerably, even
though often Churchill tried not to emphasize them unduly,
not even after the war. But what was, and remains, most important: Roosevelt realized in 1940 that Churchill was the man
who would not give in to Hitler and lose the war — while
Churchill knew that if not Roosevelt but someone like Hoover
had sat in the White House in 1940, Hitler would have won it.

* Cf. the excellent study by Christopher G. Thorne, *Allies of a Kind:
The United States, Britain, and the War Against Japan, 1941–1945,* London, 1978.

4

Churchill and Eisenhower

There were disagreements between Winston Churchill and Dwight David Eisenhower during the last year of the Second World War. There were more serious disagreements between them during the peak years of the cold war. Their relationship during the Second World War has been described by a number of military historians; during the cold war by relatively few. This is regrettable, for there is a drastic symmetry between these two periods. In 1944–1945 Eisenhower opposed Churchill's strategic advocacies, which he regarded as controversial and dangerously anti-Russian. Eight years later Eisenhower's view of the world had become the very opposite: he regarded Churchill's proposals as controversial and dangerously pro-Russian.

Most of Eisenhower's biographers argue that in 1945 Eisenhower opposed Churchill for military reasons (including the extraordinary episode when, at the end of March 1945, Eisenhower took it upon himself to bypass Churchill and wrote a direct letter to Stalin, telling him that the Allied armies, rushing forward within Germany, would not advance toward Berlin

and Prague). But there was much more than military prudence
in Eisenhower's calculations. In 1945 he was in complete conformity with what he saw as the prevalent climate of opinion
in Washington — as he would be, in 1952 and after, in complete
conformity with a different climate of opinion in Washington
then. That, I contend, was the reason for his opposition to
Churchill, on both of these occasions.

In 1945 neither Churchill nor Eisenhower could know that
less than eight years later Providence would allow them to find
themselves again in the seats of power in London and in
Washington, and that this, at first sight, fortunate circum-
stance would reveal a new kind of deep difference in their
views of the world. The evidences of these disagreements are
startling. They include their published correspondence of
1953–1955.* They reveal the existence of an, at least potentially,
missed historic opportunity, Churchill's attempt to reduce the
tensions of the cold war by establishing some kind of contact
with the then new and unsure Russian leadership in order to
ease or correct the division of Europe. They also reveal serious
flaws in Eisenhower's judgment and his character. In none of
his numerous biographies is there a substantial description of
how and why this seemingly simple (though in reality complicated and calculating) military man, with his easygoing and
liberal reputation, shed his pro-Russian and sometimes pro-
Democratic opinions to become a rigid anti-Communist, a Re-

---

*The cited excerpts from their letters are from this volume, *The
Churchill-Eisenhower Correspondence, 1953–1955,* Peter G. Boyle, ed.,
Chapel Hill, N.C., 1990.

publican, and eventually even a self-styled "conservative." But then Eisenhower's conversion only accorded with the conversion of much of American public opinion, and with a revolution in American political attitudes that began in 1947 and developed fast thereafter. In 1948 Eisenhower was still suggested for the Democratic presidential nomination; four years later he declared himself a Republican and an anti-Communist (and, during the campaign, a churchgoer — for the first time in his adult life).

Churchill returned as Prime Minister in 1951. His memories of and his trust in the British-American special relationship and wartime alliance were much stronger than any sense of bitterness that he may have had from his 1944–1945 differences with Eisenhower. He ascribed those to Eisenhower's political inexperience at the time. Churchill had preferred the Democratic to the Republican Party; he was wary of the many, often anti-British, isolationists in among the Republicans, but he took comfort in seeing his wartime comrade, a Republican internationalist, elected to the presidency. He was to be disappointed soon.

Coincidentally, the last volume of Churchill's *Second World War*, dealing with the years 1944–1945, was about to be published in 1953. In this sixth volume, *Triumph and Tragedy*, Churchill went to great lengths to underemphasize his substantial disagreements with Eisenhower in 1945. He wrote to Eisenhower on 9 April 1953: "But, now that you have assumed supreme political office in your country, I am most anxious that nothing should be published which might seem to others to threaten our current relations in our public duties or to impair the sympathy and understanding which exist between our countries. I have therefore gone over the book again in the last few months and have taken great pains to ensure that it contains nothing which might imply that there was in those days any controversy or lack of confidence between us."

Churchill wished to reestablish a good working relationship with his former wartime associate. He was worried about Eisenhower's choice of John Foster Dulles as his Secretary of State. (This was the John Foster Dulles who in June 1940, when Paris had fallen and Britain stood alone, opposed any American commitment to Britain against Hitler's Germany.)

In January 1953, before Eisenhower's inauguration, Churchill came to New York. He told Eisenhower that he was considering the possibility of a meeting with Stalin. He was aware of certain symptoms in the East. On New Year's Day in 1953 his secretary, John Colville, noted two remarkable statements by Churchill, one of which I have cited: "Churchill said that if I lived my normal span I should assuredly see Eastern Europe free of Communism. . . . Finally he lamented that owing to Eisenhower winning the Presidency he must cut much out of Volume VI of his War History and could not tell the story of how the United States gave away, to please Russia, vast tracts of Europe they had occupied and how suspicious [the Americans] then were of his pleas for caution."*

What Churchill, at that moment, did not know was how prone his former comrade again was to suspicions — partly be-

---

*John Colville, *The Fringes of Power: 10 Downing Street Diaries, 1939–1955,* New York, 1985, p. 658.

cause of his recently acquired and personally satisfying ideology, partly because of his unwillingness to displease American popular sentiment, which was reaching heights of anti-Communist hysteria around that time. Statesman that Churchill was, he probably did not understand how much of a politician was Eisenhower, a quality that some of Eisenhower's recent biographers have elevated as if that were identical with statesmanship.

On 5 March 1953, six weeks after Eisenhower's inauguration, Stalin died. There was an accumulation of information about the unsureness of the new Russian leaders and their inclination to reconsider some of their relations with the West. Six days later Churchill wrote to Eisenhower. He reminded him that "I was welcome to meet Stalin if I thought fit and that you understood this as meaning that you did not want us to go together, but now when there is no more Stalin . . . I have the feeling that we might both of us get together or separately be called to account if no attempt were made to turn over a leaf so that a new page would be started with something more coherent on it than a series of casual or dangerous incidents at the many points of contact between the two divisions of the world. I cannot doubt you are thinking deeply on this which holds first place in my thoughts."

Eisenhower did not seem to think deeply about this. He saw no difference now that Stalin was gone. "I tend to doubt the wisdom" of such a meeting, he answered, "since this would give our opponent the same kind of opportunity he often had . . . to make of the same occurrence . . . another propaganda mill for the Soviet." On 5 April, Churchill agreed that "we must remain vigilantly on our guard" and maintain the defensive rearmaments, but added that "we think, as I am sure you do also, that we ought to lose no chance of finding out how far the Malenkov regime are prepared to go in easing things up all around." He followed this up with two messages. On 11 April: "I believe myself that at this moment time is on our side." On 12 April: "It would be a pity if a sudden frost nipped spring in the bud. . . . Would it not be well to combine the re-assertions of your and our inflexible resolves with some balancing expression of hope that we have entered upon a new era?"

Eisenhower's response was short and dismissive. Churchill became somewhat impatient. On 21 April he wrote: "If nothing can be arranged I shall have to consider seriously a personal contact. You told me in New York you would have no objection to this. I should be grateful if you would let me know how these things are shaping in your mind." Eisenhower answered on 25 April: "I feel that we should not rush things too much. . . . Premature action by us in that direction might have the effect of giving the Soviets an easy way out of the position in which I think they are now placed." By this time it was obvious that Eisenhower was not only influenced but guided by John Foster Dulles (whose "great slab of a face" Churchill decried privately). Yet, wishing to demonstrate his loyalty to Eisenhower, Churchill sent him his draft of a proposed letter to Molotov, still the Russian Foreign Minister. Eisenhower rejected it. "Foster and I have considered it deeply. . . . We would advise against it. You will pardon me, I know, if I express a bit of astonishment that you think it appropriate to recommend Moscow to Molotov as a suitable meeting place. . . . Certainly nothing that the Soviet Government has done in the meantime would tend to persuade me differently."

Churchill answered two days later. "I am not afraid of the 'solitary pilgrimage' if I am sure in my heart that it may help forward the cause of peace and even at the worst can only do harm to my reputation. . . . I have a strong belief that Soviet self-interest will be their guide." Given Eisenhower's opposition, Churchill did not persist in seeking a meeting with the Russians for the time being. But in his speech on 11 May in the House of Commons — it was to be the last of his great historic speeches — Churchill spoke of his hope of finding some kind of accommodation with the new leaders of Russia. Eisenhower and Dulles dismissed him; privately Eisenhower kept referring to Churchill as "senile."

Churchill hoped to meet Eisenhower in Bermuda. Then this had to be postponed because on 23 June, Churchill had a small stroke. But his attention to American events remained acute. He was aware of the rising wave of McCarthyism. On 1 July, Senator Alexander Wiley, the Republican chairman of the Senate Committee on Foreign Relations, said that there may be a Russian change of policy, but "that is only due to fear among the trembling remnant of gangsters and felons cringing in the Kremlin." Churchill disliked such assessments. "I have no more intention than I had . . . in 1945 of being fooled by the Russians."

The Bermuda conference was now set for late November. Its very timing depended on "Foster." Eisenhower sent a message on 10 October: "Foster has gone away for the week end but, as soon as he can be contacted you will hear further from us." "Foster" now appeared in nearly every message, long or short, important or cursory, that "Ike" or "Ike E." sent to "Winston." On 7 November: "Foster will not return to Washington until the afternoon of Sunday, November 8th, the earliest." Churchill would have to wait. "This will give me the opportunity to consult with Foster." Next day Eisenhower finally agreed to a Bermuda date "because this will enable Foster to be with me." Churchill was relieved that a date was set. "All the same," he wrote, "I am, as I said last time in Parliament, hoping that we may build bridges, and not barriers." In Bermuda Dulles prevailed. There would be no top-level meeting with the Russians, only a meeting of foreign ministers on the subjects of Germany and Austria.

By early 1954 Churchill knew that his efforts to convince Eisenhower were nearly useless. Eisenhower's language in his message to Churchill on 9 February 1954 was revealing. Proclaiming "the propaganda feast the enemy enjoys at our expense," Eisenhower cited a need to "throw back the Russian threat and allow civilization, as we have known it, to continue its progress. . . . Unless [we] are successful . . . there will be no history of any kind, as we know it. There will be only a concocted story made up by the Communist conquerors of the world." This was the language, and the view of the world, of the McCarthyites at the time (and of the American "conservatives" and of the "neoconservatives" since that time).

At the end of June 1954 the seventy-nine-year-old Churchill came to Washington. He looked tired. His visit coincided with the height of the crisis of the Army-McCarthy hearings. At first Eisenhower reluctantly agreed to Churchill's proposal for a

summit, but then he changed his mind. Then Churchill gath-
ered his strength. On his way home aboard the *Queen Mary*
he drafted and sent a message to Molotov, proposing a meeting, with or without the American president. Molotov answered instantly in the affirmative. Churchill sent the letters
to Eisenhower.

"You did not let any grass grow under your feet," an obviously irritated Eisenhower reacted. "When you left here, I had
thought, obviously erroneously, that you were in an undecided
mood about this matter. . . . I shall of course have to make some
statement of my own when your plan is publicly announced. I
hope you can give me advance notice. . . . I probably shall say
something to the effect that while you were here the possibility
of a Big Three Meeting was discussed; that I could not see how
it could serve a useful purpose at this time; that I said that, if
you undertake such a mission, your plan would carry our
hopes for the best but would not engage our responsibility."
He continued in a tone that was, at least in one sense, accu-
satory: "The fact that your message to Moscow was sent so
promptly after you left here is likely to give an impression
more powerful than your cautioning words that in some way
your plan was agreed at our meeting. . . . As to the content of
Molotov's message as related in your cable, I can only observe
that it must be almost exactly what you would have expected
in the circumstances."

Churchill answered instantly. "I have made it clear to Molotov that you were in no way committed. . . . Much grass had
already grown under our feet since my telegram to you of 4
May 1953. . . . I have never varied, in the fourteen months that

have passed, from my conviction that the state of the world would not be worsened and might be helped by direct contact with the Russia which has succeeded the Stalin era. . . . I thought Molotov's reply was more cordial and forthcoming to what was after all only a personal and private enquiry than I had expected. . . . I was struck by the fact that they did not suggest a meeting in Moscow but respected my wish to leave the time and place entirely unsettled." (Later in this letter Churchill wrote: "It is my hope that an increasing detachment of Russia from Chinese ambitions may be a possibility, and one we should not neglect.")

Eisenhower would not budge. He did not think that he was wrong "in my conclusion that the men in the Kremlin are not to be trusted." Churchill wrote him instantly: "I accept full responsibility as I cannot believe that my American kinsmen will be unanimous in believing that I am either anti-American or pro-Communist." On 12 July, Eisenhower returned to "your proposed trip." He wrote that Americans would consider Churchill's effort to meet with the Russians "as Hoover is supposed to have said of Prohibition, 'a noble experiment.'" There was an element of impertinence in this phrase. And now Eisenhower went further. He engaged in an attribution of Churchill's motives. On 22 July he wrote: "I am certain that you must have a very deep and understandable desire to do something special and additional in your remaining period of active service. . . . I am sure that some such thought of your conscious or subconscious mind must be responsible for your desire to meet Malenkov." (This was addressed to the Churchill who a few months before had said that he was willing

to talk to the Russians even at the risk of "harm to my reputation.") Then Eisenhower the psychoanalyst reverted to
Eisenhower the ideologue, declaring "my utter lack of confidence in the reliability and integrity of the men in the Kremlin." Taking his time, Churchill answered on 8 August: "I am
not looking about for the means of making a dramatic exit or
of finding a suitable Curtain," he wrote. "I am however convinced that the present method of establishing the relations
between the two sides of the world by means of endless discus-
sions between Foreign Offices, will not produce any decisive
result. . . . Even when the power of Britain is so much less
than that of the United States, I feel, old age notwithstanding,
a responsibility and resolve to use any remaining influence I
may have to seek, if not for a solution at any rate for an ease-
ment. Even if nothing solid or decisive was gained no harm
need be done."

But now the tempo of the exchanges diminished; and
Churchill was preparing for his retirement. On 7 December
he wrote: "I still hope we may reach a top level meeting with
the new regime in Russia and that you and I may both be present." Eisenhower replied: "I cannot see that a top-level meeting is anything which I can inscribe on my schedule for any
predictable date." Eventually such a meeting — the first cold
war summit — would take place in Geneva in June 1955. It was
inconclusive, a useless summit.

Churchill's expectations about a meeting with the Russians
in 1953 and 1954 may or may not have been exaggerated. But
he was not often wrong about the Russians. In 1944 and 1945
he was ahead of many Americans, including Eisenhower, in

gauging the dangers of the Russian advance into Europe. From 1952 to 1955 he was ahead of Eisenhower, and of all of the cold warriors, in gauging the inevitability of Russian retreats.* Indeed, by 1955 some of these retreats had begun. The Russians withdrew from Austria, in exchange for a reciprocal removal of Western troops and a state treaty guaranteeing Austrian neutrality; they gave up their naval bases in Finland; Khrushchev was about to pay a remorseful visit to Stalin's enemy Tito in Yugoslavia. Well before that Churchill had become convinced that the appeal of Communist ideology had grown feeble, and that the bloated Soviet empire in Eastern Europe would not last.

The Churchill-Eisenhower correspondence of 1953–1955

---

* Henry Luce, the owner and editor of *Time-Life-Fortune*, was instrumental in Eisenhower's presidential nomination and election. In 1944–1945 *Time* and *Life* had been sharply critical of Churchill's anti-Communist intervention in Greece. Eight years later, in *Triumph and Tragedy*, Churchill wrote modestly: "If the editors of these well-meaning organs will look back at what they wrote then and compare it with what they think now they will, I am sure, be surprised." In the *Life* serialization of *Triumph and Tragedy* in 1953 this sentence was omitted. In 1946 *Life* wrote warily of Churchill's Iron Curtain warnings at Fulton; *Time* presented Churchill as half-potted ("Downed five Scotch highballs . . . fiddled with his speech. . . . His valet slipped him a slug of brandy to reinforce him" (*Time*, 18 March 1946). Eight years later *Time* presented him as half-doddery. "Flapping his thick arms for emphasis . . . He had not absorbed the lesson of Berlin . . . His burst of nostalgia. . . ." In a column of less than five hundred words the adjectives "old," "older," "senile," "senescent," "nostalgic," occurred nine times (*Time*, 8 March 1954).

provides ample evidence for the need to revise the lately fashionable academic approbation of Eisenhower's statesmanship. A sentence in Eisenhower's last letter to Churchill in 1955 should be sufficient to demonstrate this: "The Communist sweep over the world since World War II has been much faster and much more relentless than the 1930's sweep of the dictators." He wrote this on 29 March 1955, when the Russian retreats from Austria and Finland had already been announced; when the Russians recognized the West German government without demanding that the Western powers recognize the East German one; when the first evidences of a serious split between Russia and China had occurred; almost two years after the first popular revolt in East Berlin, and a year before the uprisings in Poland and Hungary would justify Churchill's beliefs about the indigestibility of the Russians' Eastern European domains.

In his introduction to the Churchill-Eisenhower correspondence, Boyle, a lecturer in American history at the University of Nottingham, emphasizes the cordial tone of most of these letters. Yet their reading does not justify his conclusion that "many of the long letters to Churchill provide conclusive evidence to repudiate the view that Eisenhower was a weak, ill-informed president who abrogated responsibility to others such as John Foster Dulles." They do not. Their conclusive evidence is that of a man obstinately self-satisfied with his recently acquired ideological view of the world, and extraordinarily dependent on the often wrong, and at times even sinister, advice and influence of John Foster Dulles.

We have a few scattered phrases of Churchill's contempt

for Dulles. Telling are those recorded by Churchill's personal physician Lord Moran the night of 7 December 1953, after another conference with Eisenhower in Bermuda:

> "It seems that everything is left to Dulles. It appears that the President is no more than a ventriloquist's doll."
>
> He said no more for a time. Then he said:
>
> "This fellow preaches like a Methodist Minister, and his bloody text is always the same: That nothing but evil can come out of meeting with Malenkov."
>
> There was a long pause.
>
> "Dulles is a terrible handicap." His voice rose. "Ten years ago I could have dealt with him. Even as it is I have not been defeated by this bastard. I have been humiliated by my own decay. Ah, no, Charles, you have done all that could be done to slow things down."
>
> When I turned round he was in tears.*

A terrible sadness breathes from these words. In them sits the air of an old man's self-knowledge. Churchill was tired and worn and depressed. About this his recent biographer Roy Jenkins is wrong, when he writes that Churchill "seemed curiously unfazed by [Eisenhower's and Dulles's] display of insensitivity verging on brutality." "Unfazed" he was not. But he could no longer influence these Americans; and this was not the first instance of that.

We must, however, round out the story of Churchill's Last Attempt. His wish — and vision — to seek some kind of adjust-

---

*Cited in Martin Gilbert, *Winston S. Churchill,* Boston, 1988, 8: 936.

ment with Russia was long-standing. Unlike Americans, and many others in the Western World, he understood that the Russians were weak as well as strong. His inclination to appease them was there even in the last years of Stalin's life. As early as February 1950 Churchill spoke in Edinburgh, suggesting the desirability of a parley at the "summit" (that was his word), "a supreme effort to bridge the gulf between the two worlds, so that each can live their life . . . without the hatreds of the Cold War." In December 1950 he wrote to Eisenhower (who was not yet a presidential candidate): "Appeasement from weakness and fear is . . . fatal. Appeasement from strength is magnanimous . . . and might be the surest way to peace." Negotiation from strength, from the obvious strength of the American alliance system, is what he wished to achieve, surely after Stalin's death in March 1953. With Eisenhower and Dulles he got nowhere. It was the two Dulles brothers — the Secretary of State and his brother Allen, head of the CIA — who set the course of the giant American ship of state, while Eisenhower sat in the captain's seat. Eisenhower kept repeating: Russians never change. (At Bermuda he said, "Russia is a whore.")

Still we must consider that Churchill's idea of a new approach to Russia had been rejected as early as in January 1953 by President Truman and his Secretary of State Dean Acheson in Washington. Moreover, Churchill's attempts to contact Moscow in 1953 and 1954 were also strenuously opposed by people in his own Cabinet, including Eden and Salisbury, not to speak of Chancellor Adenauer of West Germany, who saw in these attempts not much more than the wish of an old man

to close his career with a — historic, even more than diplomatic — triumph: a dangerous and headstrong attempt, propelled by vanity. That element, or factor, probably existed. But
there was more than that. Knowing some things that we know
now (including some evidence from Russian memoirs and papers), we may safely state that Churchill's vision, whether propelled by an old man's vanity or not, was not altogether wrong.

Churchill was a statesman, not an ideologue. Oddly enough,
it was Eisenhower who was the ideologue of the two — the
same Eisenhower, I repeat, who regarded Churchill as unduly dangerous because anti-Russian in 1944–1945, now regarding and treating him as dangerously senile and unduly pro-
Russian in 1953–1955. Now consider that an ideologue is not
necessarily a fanatic. What he does is adjust most of his ideas
to circumstances, without recognizing the opportunism latent
in such ideological adjustments. The opportunism of a great
statesman, on the other hand, rests on his principles. What
John Morley once wrote about Edmund Burke may be applied
to Churchill: "He changed his stand; but he never changed his
ground." Or what the aged Metternich once wrote: that an idea
is like a fixed gun in a fortress, ready to fire and to hit error
in one straight direction; but a principle is like a gun mounted
on a fixed but revolving base, capable of firing at error in all
possible directions. What mattered for Eisenhower were current ideas. What mattered for Churchill were certain principles. Eisenhower's view of the world, and of its inhabitants,
was political. Churchill's was historical. They may have seen
their opponents differently: but underneath all of that lay the
difference in their characters.

5

Churchill, Europe, and appeasement

Much has been written about Churchill and "appeasement," not much (except indirectly) about Churchill and "Europe." It is my contention that these two themes — two preoccupations of his mind in crucial times — were not only connected but inseparable. He would not accept a British acquiescence in Germany's dominating Europe. He saw that prospect earlier than had others, whence his strident struggle against the appeasement of Hitler's Third Reich during the 1930s. That is not arguable. What is arguable is his attitude toward Europe throughout his life. After all, Britain's alliance with the United States was often his priority. After all, he — like most of his countrymen — thought, at least often, that the Channel was wider than the Atlantic. After all, he hoped for, and tried to promote, some kind of a unity among the English-speaking peoples, but not a British association, let alone a confederation, with a European union.

But that was not all. Certainly he was no British isolationist. In 1889 Lord Salisbury said: "There is all the difference in the world between good-natured, good-humoured effort to keep well with your neighbors, and that spirit of haughty and sullen isolation which has been dignified with the name of non-intervention. We are part of the community of Europe, and we must do our duty as such." Churchill would have agreed to that. Such was his conviction throughout his life. He had entered his public and parliamentary career when the entente cordiale with France was concluded, in 1904. About that Andrew Roberts, Salisbury's excellent biographer, wrote that "barely a year after Salisbury's death, [the entente cordiale] linked British fortunes to those of a country which turned out to be in faster relative decline during the first half of the twentieth century than even Britain herself."* But what alternative did Britain have? Recently, near the end of the twentieth century, a few people suggested and the British historian Niall Fergusson wrote that Britain would have done better to accept a German-dominated and perhaps thus united Europe and not to have entered the European war in 1914 on the side of Belgium and France. That is an argument that I think Churchill would have dismissed (and, were he alive, he would still dismiss) with a quick and angry flick of his cigar.

He was in favor of the entente with France from the beginning. (It would be interesting to know what the sources of his cultural Francophilia were; when and where did they begin? — another topic for further research.) His pro-Americanism was not in conflict with that. For in the background of the British decision to proceed to an understanding with France there

---

*Andrew Roberts, *Salisbury: Victorian Titan*, London, 1999, pp. 488, 843.

was an American element: the British decision, in and after 1898, near-universal among its people, sometimes unspoken but profound, not to risk any confrontation with the United States, to keep and maintain the best possible relations with the emerging transatlantic giant, still a blood relative of sorts. Only with this kind of security in the back could Britain engage in the effort to arrange European support against a potential confrontation with Germany.

Of course Churchill was also impressed with the record of British armies in great wars fought on the continent of Europe, including those waged by his ancestor Marlborough: a series of battle names, ranging from Blenheim, Ramillies, Malplaquet through Corunna, Badajoz, Salamanca, Waterloo (and perhaps even Sevastopol). He had educated himself well; in any case, his knowledge of European history and geography was more than considerable. We know that he admired England's two greatest French opponents, Joan of Arc and Napoleon. But this amounted to more than a sentimental or romantic Francophilia. In 1914 there was more than a warrior's temperament that convinced him how Britain could not but be involved in the fast-coming European war. His description of what happened late in the afternoon of 24 July, near the end of the Buckingham Palace Conference preoccupied with the problem of Ireland reflects that reality, impressionist and lyrical as that description is. The meeting had been inconclusive, the participants were tired, when a paper was brought to Sir Edward Grey, with the terms of the Austrian ultimatum to Serbia. "The parishes of Fermanagh and Tyrone faded back into the mists and squalls of Ireland, and a strange light began immediately, but by perceptible gradations, to fall and grow upon the map of Europe."* The map of Europe: that lit up Churchill's eyes, immediately.

Did he realize, soon after the war, what the bleeding and broken mosaic of the new Europe, largely due to the victory of the wearied and often thoughtless Allies, meant and would mean? Yes and no — or, rather: yes rather than no. Immediately after the war his main preoccupations and actions concerned Bolshevism in Russia and Ireland and the Middle East. His wish to promote an ever closer British relationship with the United States seldom appeared during the twenties. None of his official posts or even parliamentary concerns had much to do with Europe then. Yet he was thinking — and writing — much about Europe, about its then present and mutable conditions, and about its future. As early as November 1918 he said in the Cabinet: "We might abandon Europe but Europe will not abandon us." Immediately after the war he spoke up against mistreating the German people (as he would also do after the Second World War). He welcomed the Treaty of Locarno in 1925. At that very time he was writing the second volume of his own history of the First World War. Sometime in 1926 (*The World Crisis, 1916–1918* was published in January 1927) he ended it with these ringing words: "Is this the end? Is it to be merely a chapter in a cruel and senseless story? Will a new generation in their turn be immolated to square the black accounts of Teuton and Gaul? Will our children bleed and

*Winston Churchill, *The World Crisis, 1911–1918,* abridged, London, 1931, p. 110.

gasp again in devastated lands? Or will there spring from the very fires of conflict that reconciliation of the three giant combatants, which would unite their genius and secure to each in safety and freedom a share in rebuilding the glory of Europe?"

What appears from these words is Churchill's certainty that a dreadful future struggle between Germany and France ("Teuton and Gaul") would naturally and inevitably include Britain too — a view not in the least shared by his British contemporaries at that time. Significant is his rhetorical ending, a hope for a prospective unity, "a share in rebuilding the glory of Europe." The prospect of a united Europe appealed to Churchill. He wrote and spoke about it often during the twenties. In 1923 the Austrian-born cosmopolitan nobleman Count Richard Coudenhove-Kalergi launched his "Pan-Europe" movement, followed by a considerable resonance. Churchill supported it; so did, cautiously, the then-leading European statesmen, Briand and Stresemann. In Coudenhove-Kalergi's plan neither Britain nor Russia would be part of a European union: Churchill agreed with that. At the same time he welcomed the plan for some kind of European union emphatically (again, almost alone among British politicians). In February 1930 he wrote in an American publication: "We see nothing but good and hope in a richer, freer, more contented European commonalty. But we have our own dream and our task. We are with Europe but not of it. We are linked but not committed. We are interested and associated, but not absorbed."* Significant, too, are his occasional statements and writings

*Saturday Evening Post, 15 February 1930.

about what he saw as the most dangerous places and problems situated on the new map of Europe: he would mention Danzig, and Transylvania.

And his eyes were on Europe even before Hitler became the leader of a new Germany, in the early thirties when Churchill was politically embroiled — deeply and vocally, with considerable harm to his reputation — in what should happen with India, and when (as we shall see in the next chapter) he had and spoke his doubts about the very viability of parliamentary democracy and of universal suffrage. We have seen how, surprising his German hosts, Churchill spoke at a diplomatic dinner about his concern with Hitler in October 1930, at a time when no one else in the world (except, of course, for Hitler himself), including Germany, would ever envision Hitler as a future leader of Germany. But even before Hitler came into power there was growing evidence of a Germany feeling its oats, even though struggling through the worst kind of economic depression. The evidence is there in the disarmament conferences of 1931 and 1932, with German demands ratcheted up higher and higher. Churchill understood what that meant. "Germany Arming!" he declaimed — perhaps exaggeratedly so. Again and again he emphasized the importance of the French army — not because of his Francophile or sentimental inclinations: he saw the French army as the only possible serious counterweight against Germany's rising power and arms.

Churchill's warnings and his struggle against the "appeasement" of Germany have often been analyzed and described as if his main concern had been the military unpreparedness of Britain. (There are several valuable analyses comparing his estimates of British and German aircrafts and aircraft building which now seem to have been inaccurate, though not entirely wrong.) But we must consider that his fighting against appeasement, while concerned with the wanting state of British military preparedness, was at least equally, if not more, concerned with the developing state of Europe. These two cardinal matters were of course inseparable. But: had there been no evidence of an increasing German preponderance in the center of Europe, the state of British armaments would have mattered less: it would have been secondary, if not altogether marginal. Conversely: had British rearmament reached a satisfactory, or even impressive, stage in the 1930s, the importance of that condition would have been secondary to the importance of a Third German Reich dominating more and more of Europe. There were many Englishmen, including some of Churchill's friends, who did not see things in that way. Some of them even believed that the very presence of a new Germany was a welcome factor against Communism. Among them was Lord Rothermere, who had met Hitler and then received an impressive letter from him in 1935, which he showed to Churchill. Churchill's answer was: "If his [Hitler's] proposal means that we should come to an understanding with Germany to dominate Europe, I think this would be contrary to the whole of our history." *The whole of our history* . . . Thus the Europe-minded Tory Churchill, in contrast to his conservative (and still imperial-minded) isolationists . . .

Appeasement and *appeasers*. Looking back from the twenty-first century we may see that the meaning of these terms changed twice during the past sixty-five years. On 9 March

1936 (note that this was but two days after Hitler, dismissing the Locarno Treaty, had marched into the demilitarized portion of the Rhineland) Anthony Eden spoke in the Commons: "It is the appeasement of Europe as a whole that we have constantly before us." Perhaps this was the first time that the word *appeasement* appeared, at that time employed in a positive sense. Two years later Eden became one of the antiappeasers. In less than another year appeasement acquired its negative connotation, which it still maintains. Yet the motives of the appeasers of the 1930s were not, and ought not to be seen, as irresponsible. There were three main elements in their inclinations, words, policies, acts. One was the wish to avoid war, an honest wish fortified by the memories of the carnage less than twenty years before. It had a particular component: not to see Britain involved in a potential, let alone actual, war in Europe. The other was an outcome of British fairmindedness: the slow movement of belief, reaching its zenith in the mid-thirties, that Germany had been treated unfairly by the Versailles Treaty and that, consequently or not, Germany deserved a benefit of doubt. The third element was anti-Communism, of which Hitler was the chief spokesman and proponent. After all, Communism was now extirpated in Germany, a nation that had become a bulwark against Soviet Russia and International Communism. When Neville Chamberlain succeeded Stanley Baldwin as Prime Minister in 1937, there was an additional element within his inclinations: a distrust of France, together with the willingness to extend more than a modicum of the benefit of doubt to the new Germany (an inclination that his brother Austen would not have shared but that his father Joseph Chamberlain, who in 1899 had proposed an Anglo-Saxon-Teutonic alliance to govern most of the world, might well have). In Chamberlain's mind, and in the minds of many Conservatives, these inclinations contributed to a tendency to regard most reports about the brutalities and conditions of the Hitler regime as exaggerations and propaganda.

These inclinations, maturing into acts, policies, and decisions, may have been shortsighted; but they were not irresponsible, and certainly not disreputable. Until March 1939 they were largely in accord with the sentiments and opinions of many, if not most, of the British people. As early as 23 March 1936 Harold Nicolson wrote in his diary: "The feeling in the House is terribly pro-German" — perhaps an exaggeration, but not much. The biographer of King George V, Kenneth Rose, summed up the case against appeasement well: "What tarnishes the memory of the so-called appeasers is not that they were deterred from robustness by the strategic and economic realities of a defence policy; it is the sycophancy with which they witnessed the creeping enslavement of Europe."* Europe . . . On 11 June 1937 (a relatively calm year) Churchill wrote: "How has it all gone in Europe while we have been thinking about our own affairs? I, personally, have never been able to forget Europe. It hangs over my mind." As Robert Rhodes James wrote: "He had been fighting his campaign less against

*Kenneth Rose, *King George V*, New York, 1984, p. 86.

an Administration than against a national temper." This of course involved the Press Lords, including Rothermere (a friend) and Beaverbrook (who was to become close to Churchill only years later). In 1935 Churchill wrote: "There would be a great deal to be said for [Beaverbrook's] policy of a pacific isolationism if we could only arrange to have the United Kingdom towed out fifteen hundred miles into the Atlantic." Evidently Churchill did not always see the Channel as wider than the Atlantic. In James's words, he "saw and felt something that few other contemporaries did — that the world was in the presence of a terrible personal and national phenomenon for which there has been no parallel since Napoleon"* — indeed, worse than Napoleon. In an otherwise unexceptionable and readable essay about "Churchill the Statesman" A. J. P. Taylor writes that Churchill "had no vision of a new Europe, still less of a new world. He wanted to get back to the old one."†

This is not convincing. In an excellent book, *Churchill and Appeasement*, R. A. C. Parker illustrates that Chamberlain's policy to appease Hitler was not simply due to a shrewd and prudent decision to gain time for rearmament. This is important. It is true that while Chamberlain was engaged in pursuing appeasement he was also engaged in British rearmament, especially in the air. But let me add: there is not the slightest

* Cited by Robert Rhodes James, *Churchill: A Study in Failure, 1900–1939*, New York, 1970, pp. 308, 311, 318.

† A. J. P. Taylor, "The Statesman," in *Churchill Revised: A Critical Assessment*, New York, 1969, p. 36.

indication, or evidence, that after having reached a satisfactory stage of rearmament, Chamberlain and the appeasers would then have changed their course to a stiff opposition to Hitler. There was, as mentioned earlier, also Chamberlain's Russophobia and Francophobia and anti-Communism.

Churchill was certainly anti-Communist. But it was the prospect of a German-ruled Europe that was foremost in his mind. He said in January 1937 to the Leeds Chamber of Commerce (which had invited Ribbentrop, then the German ambassador to Britain, who could not come, and they had to make do with Churchill) that what Hitler believed (in part as an implication of the Anglo-German naval agreement of 1935) was that Britain should abandon a goodly part of Europe, certainly Central and most of Eastern Europe, to Germany. Churchill understood Hitler very well, which turned out to be an incomparable asset. Whether a Churchill in power in the thirties could have prevented the expansion of the Third Reich is certainly arguable — contrary to what he wrote in *The Gathering Storm*, the first volume of his *The Second World War*. What is not arguable is that the essential difference between him and the appeasers (a difference that, in many ways, prevailed until July 1940) was his conviction that the fate of Britain was not and could not be separated from the fate of Europe. His Conservative adversaries knew less of Europe than he did; and they were suspicious of English ties and commitments to Europe. This contributed to their lacking comprehension of Hitler's purposes and of his power. They did not understand that if his Germany were allowed to dominate all of Central and most of Eastern Europe, the independence of the Western Euro-

pean democracies, including France, would be fatefully compromised and fatefully constrained: that what was at stake was
more than any traditional arrangement of balance of power.

Here we come to a significant matter which has been
brought up lately by some of Churchill's critics, direct or indi-
rect. This is Churchill's statement within the secrecy of the
War Cabinet, on 26 May 1940, during the five days when he
had to fight against Halifax's advocacy of cautious negotiations. The evidence comes from those minutes and from
Chamberlain's diary. "The P. M. disliked any move toward
Musso." (Halifax had argued to explore whether Mussolini
could — eventually — mediate, that is, ascertain under what
terms Hitler would agree to a cessation of the war.) Chamberlain quoted Churchill: "It was incredible that Hitler would
consent to any terms that we could accept — though if we could
get out of this jam by giving up Malta & Gibraltar & some African colonies he would jump at it." This has been frequently
cited by Churchill's critics, with the purpose of demonstrating
that, after all, the accepted (and Churchill's own) portrait of his
uncompromising, bulldog determination is, to say the least,
inaccurate. But the essence of the matter was not his single-
mindedness. It was his understanding of Hitler: his knowledge, both rational and intuitive, that (a) any British indication
even to explore negotiations at that dire moment would fatefully strengthen Hitler's hand; (b) that Hitler's terms would
amount to the reduction of Britain to, at worst, a satellite, at
best, a junior and consenting partner of Germany, including
a definite British commitment to accord with and live next to
a Germany ruling Europe. He said, again within the secrecy

of the War Cabinet on 27 May: "If Herr Hitler was prepared to make peace on the terms of the restoration of German colonies and the overlordship of Central Europe, that was one thing. But it was quite unlikely that he would make any such offer." In May 1940 Hitler wanted to get more than that: the mastery of all Europe, with Britain agreeing, or forced to agree.

So Churchill wrote to Roosevelt on 15 June 1940, including this sentence: "If we go down, you may have a United States of Europe under the Nazi command far more numerous, far stronger, far better armed than the New World." It was thus that on 14 July he declared that Britain was fighting "*by* ourselves alone, but not *for* ourselves alone" (also that London now "was this strong City of Refuge which enshrines the title-deeds of human progress and is of deep consequence to Christian civilization"). He did not for a moment believe that Britain and the Empire could continue to exist across from a Europe entirely ruled by Germany.

Not enough attention has been directed to Churchill's vision of Europe during the war. Yes: he saw that if the price of the survival of British independence and of British democracy was the eventual transference of much of the imperial burden to the Americans, so be it; yes, the maintenance and the development of his alliance with America was his priority. Yet it was in one of his broadcasts to the United States in 1941 that he said: "In these British Islands that look so small on the map we stand, the faithful guardians of the right and dearest hopes of a dozen States and nations now gripped and tormented in a base and cruel servitude." In the last pages of *Five Days in London, May 1940,* I wrote: "His phrases about London having become the custodian of Western civilization were not mere rhetoric: there was the presence of the exiled kings and queens of Western Europe in its mansions, there was the colorful presence of their uniformed soldiers and sailors in its streets (including the brave Poles, thousands of them); there were those Bach concerts in its darkened Victorian halls — and the British Broadcasting Corporation's signal opening its European broadcasts with the first bar of Beethoven's Fifth Symphony." Churchill, Maurice Ashley wrote, "remained at heart a European and hoped that the Americans would treasure, above all, their European heritage."* When in November 1944 General de Gaulle tried to wean him away from his close dependence on the United States and in a European direction, Churchill said that he understood de Gaulle's argument and agreed with much of it: but the primacy of his relationship with America must and would prevail. At the same time his concern with Europe, including the prospects of a postwar Europe, remained more than considerable.

It influenced his propositions of strategy. Invading and liberating Europe from the south, and his subsequent plans for landing in the western Balkans or pushing from Italy northeastward, were to precede, or then complement, the invasion of Western Europe, but there was another purpose, too: to establish an Anglo-American presence in at least portions of Central Europe, forestalling the Russian occupation of its entirety. Until mid-1943 he was able to influence his American allies, with the result of going into Sicily and the Italian main-

* Maurice Ashley, *Churchill as Historian*, New York, 1968, p. 209.

land; thereafter no longer: they rejected his Adriatic plans for
a number of reasons, one of these being their suspicion of
Churchill's interest in parts of Europe where Americans were
loath to be involved. But Churchill's concern with Europe
went beyond his advocacies of military strategy. It was evident
in his proposition (at Teheran) for an independent Austria; in
his plans for an eventual South German–Austrian postwar
state, perhaps even including Hungary; in his Percentages
proposition to Stalin, which amounted to more than the saving
of Greece, with Churchill willing to accept the Russian domination of Rumania and Bulgaria, for which there were historic
precedents, and where the Russians were already the occu-
pying forces de facto; we have also seen that he would state,
on occasion, that Hungary was not an Eastern but a Central
European state. But in his concern about how far the Russians
would advance into Central Europe he had no American
help — rather the contrary.

Then, during the last months of the war in Europe his energy was weakening. He would still state his concerns clearly;
but his persistence in following them up was not what it had
been before. True — as the war went on, he had fewer cards
in his hand. Yet there were some that were there and that he
did not play. One was a, somewhat vague, idea current in
Whitehall and even brought up by Eden in late 1944, for a
Western European alliance system under British leadership.
I have often thought that in 1945 the British, including
Churchill, missed a great historic chance. They could have
gotten the leadership of all Western Europe for a song. Such
was their prestige among the liberated Western European and

Scandinavian peoples, a solid prestige that was principally due to Churchill's wartime leadership (and also to the fact that these countries had been liberated mostly by British and Commonwealth armies). But at that time the wearied British people and their representatives were — understandably — uninterested in any such project; and so was Churchill. Perhaps, had he been reelected in July 1945, things may have been different. But because of many conditions — including the political and economic constraints of his country, and also his personal constraints of aging and health — that may not have happened at all.

Still: Churchill remained a principal proponent of a united Europe. Note, again, that his famous Iron Curtain speech at Fulton in March 1946 emphasized not the danger of International Communism but the division of Europe — the rising concern among Americans was the former; Churchill's concern was, rather, the latter — in sum, what the Russian suppression of ancient European states and their enforced isolation from the rest of Europe meant. In this concern with Eastern Europe he was alone among all the statesmen of the Western world, even including such impressive men as President Truman and General de Gaulle. A few months later, in Zurich (a speech that almost sixty years later is still remembered by many thoughtful Europeans), he raised the spectre of a desirable unity of Europe, resting first and foremost on a new kind of reconciliation and association between the French and German peoples. "His language about Europe was so warm in these years that it is easy to misunderstand what other affections cohabited with it in that capacious mind. At

Zurich, he began with a rendering of the well-educated European's hymn to the excellence of his inheritance."* He spoke in such terms at a European Union Congress at The Hague in 1948, and also on other occasions. Yet even during the second time of his Prime Ministership he did little or nothing to promote a British connection with the Western European states and with their then developing European institutions across the Channel. In 1950 he said: "We are *with* Europe, but not *in* Europe." He continued to regard the rigid division of Europe as the main factor of the cold war; in 1949 he said in Brussels: "The Europe we seek to unite is *all* Europe"; his attempt to parley with the new leaders of Russia in 1953 and 1954 had as its main purpose a correction or a mitigation of that condition; but we saw how he was rebuffed by Eisenhower and by other Americans. He was now near the very end of his political life. Yet, remarkably, he still spoke in favor of a united Europe on occasion – for instance at Aachen, in 1956, where he said that the unity of Western Europe was desirable, because it was

*"I wish to speak to you today about the tragedy of Europe. This noble continent, comprising the fairest and the most cultivated regions of the earth, enjoying a temperate and equable climate, is the home of all of the great parent races of the western world. It is the fountain of Christian faith and Christian ethics. It is the origin of most of the culture, arts, philosophy and science both of ancient and modern times. If Europe were once united in the sharing of its common inheritance, there would be no limit to [its] happiness." Quoted by Geoffrey Best, *Churchill: A Study in Greatness*, London, 2001, p. 278. Yet Best adds: "But nowhere in the speech or at any time later did he take the opportunity to insist that Britain was a European country in the full sense that the continental ones were."

consequent to such unity that the states of Eastern Europe would regain their independence, an inevitable development that he foresaw years earlier.

He did not live to see the developing predicament of Britain's associations with "Europe." I doubt that a faceless, frequently powerless, largely bureaucratic "European Union" would meet his approval; but I think that he would have welcomed the Chunnel trains.

"Churchill and Europe" is a book still to be written. It was while I was preparing the writing of this chapter that I found something quite remarkable. On 2 January 2002, the day after the adoption of the Euro through much of Europe, I read in a newspaper a list of interviews with prominent Europeans: Frenchmen, Italians, Dutch, Swiss, and others. One of the questions posed to them was this: who, to them, were the greatest Europeans? Their answers included such diverse people as Leonardo da Vinci or Jean Monnet: but, to my surprise — and joy — at least three of them listed Winston Churchill. Few if any Englishmen would consider Churchill as a great "European"; yet the choice of these Europeans was not shortsighted — rather, the contrary.

6

Churchill's historianship

Churchill was a writer. Was he a born writer? We cannot tell, except to say that the talent of a writer is seldom hereditary. That talent may, of course, develop by the example of a parent. Yet the impulse to write is one of self-expression. The motive to write is the desire to vanquish a mental preoccupation by expressing it consciously and clearly, while the purpose to write almost always contains self-centeredness and at least a minimum of vanity. I dare to think that these (I know: arguable) generalizations apply to Winston Churchill.

He was a writer. Was he a historian? There are many academics who are wont to deny that title to him: an amateur, no member of their guild; some of them (not merely professional but ideological critics) imputing that his methods of historianship were unscientific and insufficient (or, worse, self-serving and myth-making). That is one extreme. Entirely contrary to that is the commonsense assertion that every human being is a historian by nature while he is a scientist only by choice, historicity being the fourth dimension of man. However: not many men and women are conscious of that condition; few of

them experience the need to write any kind of history; and
even fewer make their writing of history not only "scientific"
but works of art. Churchill did so: whence, in all probability,
his award of the Nobel Prize for literature (in 1953, and in a
country where most professional historians were still inclined
to regard history as a Science). But then he was in good com-
pany (although he did not travel to Stockholm for the ceremony): the only other historian who had received the Nobel
Prize for Literature was the great German historian Theodor
Mommsen in 1902.

In a stately (and plummy) essay J. H. Plumb writes that
Churchill "was a rare and singular hybrid: a writer-statesman
and a statesman-writer."* I would prefer: a historian-states-
man and a statesman-historian. Churchill was a writer mainly
because he was attracted to history, not a historian because
he was attracted to writing. (Plumb, as we shall see, gives ade-
quate and even moving tribute to Churchill's overwhelming
sense of history, but is critical of Churchill's historianship.)
To the best of my knowledge only one full-size volume exists
about Churchill the historian, written by his once assistant
Maurice Ashley; other assessments of Churchill's historianship may be found in articles and addresses by Robert
Blake, Victor Feske, John Ramsden, David Reynolds.† I think

* J. H. Plumb, "The Historian," in *Churchill Revised: A Critical Assessment*. New York, 1969, p. 143.

† Robert Blake, "Winston Churchill as Historian," lecture in 1990 at
the University of Texas, rpt. in W. Roger Louis, ed., *Adventures with
Britannia: Personalities, Politics, and Culture in Britain*, Austin, 1995. Victor Feske, *From Belloc to Churchill: Private Scholars, Public Culture, and*

that (like "Churchill and Europe") a substantial book about "Churchill as Historian" is yet to be written.

One difficulty for such a work would be that the volume and the scope of Churchill's histories is enormous. But before I turn to a necessarily brief and certainly inadequate summary description and occasional analysis of his principal books, I think I must say something about his own perspective of his historianship. I think that this deserves interest, not only because it has been seldom analyzed by historians but also because (at least in my opinion) there is an element in that perspective which is not old-fashioned or traditional but perhaps surprisingly timely.

Churchill's perspective in many of his books is participatory. I said earlier that the purpose to write is seldom separable from self-centeredness. There are many historians (perhaps especially those who categorize their craft as being a Science, not an Art)* who would prefer not to think of this condition — even though the very choice of their subjects of study is usually inseparable from their personal curiosity or interest. To admit self-centeredness is of course to admit that the ideal of scien-

---

the Crisis of British Liberalism, 1900–1939, Chapel Hill, 1996. John Ramsden, " 'That Will Depend on Who Writes the History': Winston Churchill as His Own Historian," Queen Mary and Westfield College, London, 1996. David Reynolds, "Churchill's Writing of History: Appeasement, Autobiography, and *The Gathering Storm,*" in *Transactions of the Royal Historical Society,* series 6, vol. XI, Cambridge, 2001, pp. 221–247.

*Veronica Wedgwood's excellent formulation: "History is an art — like all the other sciences." I think Churchill would have agreed.

tific objectivity is wanting. Yet we, at least beyond the twentieth century and perhaps of the entire so-called Modern Age,
ought to know that the ideal of Objectivity, meaning a complete, and antiseptic, separation of the observer from the matter observed, is impossible (and not only in the mental but also
in the physical world); that the alternative to Objectivity is *not*
Subjectivity (which is but another form of determinism); that
all human knowledge is inevitably personal and participatory.
Almost all of Churchill's written work illustrates this. Almost
all of his books were inspired and researched and written because of his preoccupation with and his consequent interest
in the history of people who were intimately related to him,
and in historical events in which he was a participant. Thus
his histories of the Indian and Sudan wars, thus the political
biography of his father, thus the historical biography of his
ancestor Marlborough, thus his histories of the First World
War, of the Second World War, thus even his portraits of his
contemporaries and, at least indirectly, of his history of the
English-speaking peoples, the propagation of an idea whereof
he was a principal proponent nearly throughout his life. (Exceptions could have been biographies of Garibaldi and of Napoleon that he once thought he might write.)

Personal and participatory: these adjectives sum up the historical philosophy inherent in Winston Churchill's writings. It
is wrong to attribute this simply to the method of an amateur.
Besides the argument that in history, unlike in many of the
natural and applied sciences, *amateur* and *professional* are not
and cannot be entirely separate and distinct categories,
Churchill was aware of the conditions and limitations of his

historianship. At the beginning of his massive history of the First World War, *The World Crisis* (1923–1927), he wrote: "I set myself at each stage to answer the questions: 'What happened, and why?' I seek to guide the reader to those points where the course of events is being decided, whether it be on a battle-field, in a conning tower, in Council, in Parliament, in a lobby, a laboratory or a workshop. *Such a method is no substitution for history, but it may be an aid both to the writing and to the study of history*" (my italics). Such an admission ought at least miti-gate the bite of the witty remark made, I think, by Balfour, that Churchill had written a big book about himself and then called it *The World Crisis*. Churchill could be self-critical, at least on occasion. About *The World Crisis* he wrote: "Looking back with after-knowledge and increasing years, I seem to have been too ready to undertake tasks which were hazardous or even for-lorn." In his first (and sometimes properly criticized) volume of *The Second World War* he wrote about the thirties: "I strove my utmost to galvanise the Government into vehemence and extraordinary preparation, even at the cost of world alarm. In these endeavours no doubt I painted the picture even darker than it was." In the preface to *The Second World War* he in-sisted again: "I do not describe it as history, for that belongs to another generation. But I claim with confidence that it is a contribution to history which will be of service to the future."

There are historians who may tend to dismiss that qualifica-tion "a contribution to history" as insincere or false modesty; but they will ignore his writing and his materials, "of service to the future," only at their peril. It should also be noted that while, for all kinds of reasons, Churchill omitted or toned down certain matters of controversy, including instances when he had been right and his opponents wrong, often he did not omit a record of his words and acts that at the time of publication would raise eyebrows, to say the least (as in the case of his descriptions of Stalin and of his dealings with him). In the prefaces of both of his world war histories he wrote that he followed, "as far as I am able, the method of Defoe's *Memoirs of a Cavalier,* in which the author hangs the chronicle and discussion of great military and political events upon the thread of the personal experiences of an individual." That method (or, rather, structure and perspective) was then complemented, in almost all of his works, by copious, and sometimes too extensive, reproductions of letters and directives and other papers for the purposes of documentary illustration, suggesting at least an amateur historian's respect for the professional canon of dependence on "primary" sources.

Many of these documents inserted in his text, illustrating (but also occasionally interrupting) his narrative or his argumentation, are very valuable. They are also evidences of his assiduous attempts at research. Observe, however, that many of his books were long — often too long. His speeches were seldom long-winded. His writings — with some exceptions and of course with the exception of his journalism — often were. There was a tendency (as we saw before, in many of his important letters and messages) to expect much from his written record: Try to tell everything. And well!

His interest in — more: his appetite for — history matured very early. He was twenty-one years old and in India when he asked his mother to send him twelve volumes of Macaulay (eight of his histories, four of his collected essays). He wrote to her that he read fifty pages of Macaulay and twenty-five of Gibbon every day. "Macaulay is easier reading than Gibbon, and in quite a different style. Macaulay crisp and forcible, Gibbon stately and impressive. Both are fascinating and show what a fine language English is since it can be pleasing in styles so different."* They had an influence on his style. But he was already a writer (and a journalist: he was not yet twenty-two when he wrote and sold five articles to *The Daily Graphic*). And then came, soon, five volumes of Churchillian — that is, participatory and contemporary — history: *The Story of the Malakand Field Force* (1898), *The River War* (two volumes, 1899); *Savrola* (1900, his only novel and one written in a hurry); *London to Ladysmith* (1900); *Ian Hamilton's March* (1900). Five books written and published within three years, before he was twenty-six; and what eventful years those were, including his war in the Sudan, and then in South Africa, his capture by the Boers, and his escape. This is not the occasion to describe or analyze them in any detail. They were not long; many of them were rewritings of some of his journalist's dispatches. Eventually they became superseded by his incomparable memoir, *My Early Life: A Roving Commission* (1930), probably the most delightful book he wrote, summing up in a few short and sparkling chapters his own history of those years and adventures.

His talents for historical reconstruction are detectable in these early books (the first of them was already so recognized in a review in the *Athenaeum:* "a military classic"). Yet even

*Randolph Churchill, *Winston S. Churchill,* 1: 327–328.

more significant are those glimpses of his historical vision (and political thinking) that appear, here and there, in those early books. We have seen one visionary passage earlier, a vision perhaps comparable to the other, more famous dark vision of a contemporary, Kipling's poem "Recessional" in 1897. In his novel *Savrola* we may glimpse his conditional appreciation of a dictator, together with his melancholy perspective of mass democracy (or, rather, populism). At the end of his first book he wrote this about his own people, the British: "a people of whom at least it may be said that they have added to the happiness, the learning and the liberties of mankind." These are the words of a patriot — though not of a nationalist. (Hitler said often, and wrote in *Mein Kampf,* that he was a nationalist: "but not a patriot.")

In 1902 Churchill turned to the writing of one of his most substantial works, the life of his father. *Lord Randolph Churchill,* "a political biography," consisted of two massive volumes, more than one thousand pages *in toto*. Such extensive political biographies were not unusual at that time, though this Victorian custom was beginning to fade. What was unusual was that most of these two volumes deal with but six agitated years of his father's career, 1880 to 1886. It is obvious that the son's inspiration and purpose was a vindication of his father. This is remarkable, perhaps especially because the son did not see his father often; their relationship was not a very close one; and the father died before his son reached twenty-one. There is also remarkably little about their family life (and, except for a few letters, very little about the relationship of Lord and Lady Randolph). And then, while Lord Randolph was certainly in-

teresting, he was not altogether an attractive personality. He
was a great speaker, he spoke easily (unlike his son, who had
to prepare his speeches and even his pronunciation carefully),
but he had many a prejudice* and strong inclinations to dema-
goguery† (which his son had not). Joseph Chamberlain and
Randolph Churchill were principally responsible for destroying Gladstone's humane (and, at that time, perhaps workable)
proposition of Home Rule for Ireland. He had a very quick
mind, he was impatient (like his son); he was a maverick and
at times a rebel within his own party — most of the Conservatives did not like him (again as the case of his son); he resigned
from an important Cabinet post because of his unyielding
principles (as asserted in the biography written by his son) but
also in a huff (as asserted by his contemporary adversaries and
critics). In 1888 certain newspapers would describe Randolph
Churchill as "a boastful, rattling egotist with no principle and,
apparently, with no conception of duty and honour" (2: 358).
(Such very phrases and words were to be applied to his son
often, at least during the first sixty-four years of his life.)

Yet: if a *grand plaidoyer*, as a vindication *Lord Randolph
Churchill* does not succeed, as a great political history it does.
There have been critics who declared it a masterpiece, some
of them perhaps the finest book Winston Churchill had writ-

---

*One example, his letter to his wife from Lourdes: "a monument to
the *bêtise humaine*." R. Churchill, *Winston S. Churchill*, 2: 436.

† His visit to Belfast, after his violent pro-Ulster speeches, was followed by a riot at which at least twenty-five people (mostly Catholics)
were killed and hundreds injured.

ten. The circumstances of its composition are interesting enough. Churchill had some trouble to allow his father's literary executors to get access to all of his father's voluminous papers and correspondence. He especially needed the help of Lord Rosebery, which the latter gave, albeit a little reluctantly. Unlike his writing of his first rapidly composed and compiled books, Churchill worked four hard years on this one. (He did have some exceptional help: one of his cousins put him up at Blenheim while he was working there on his father's papers; another cousin let him work in a fine apartment in London.)* And the literary qualities of the book are often exceptional. It begins with a beautifully written and deeply evocative description of Blenheim. (Rosebery advised Churchill to omit this. Fortunately he didn't.) His critics have often deprecated Churchill for having been self-educated, an autodidact: but how rich are the evidences of his reading and learning in this political biography! The epigraph he chose for it is from Goethe (odd for a man accused of knowing little and caring little for Germany and its culture); other epigraphs of chapters and other superb quotations abound from Machiavelli, Horace, Burke, Disraeli, Crabbe, Dryden, the Book of Job. Scattered through the book's pages is a treasury of memorable phrases and descriptions. Perhaps more important: *Lord Randolph Churchill* is an extraordinarily valuable — and enduring — contribution to British political history during the mid-1800s,

---

*He was well paid for this book. It is interesting to note that his literary agent was Frank Harris, the same Harris who later became famous for his crudely sexual autobiography.

which in many ways was a turning point. About that let me cite the young Churchill's brilliant and grave description of that history at that time:

> There were important measures. There were earnest, ambitious men. But something more lay behind the unrest and uncertainties of the day. Not merely the decay of Government or the natural over-ripeness of a party produced the agitations of 1885 and 1886. The long dominion of the middle classes, which had begun in 1832, had come to its close and with it the almost equal reign of Liberalism. The great victories had been won. All sorts of lumbering tyrannies had been toppled over. Authority was everywhere broken. Slaves were free. Conscience was free. Trade was free. But hunger and squalor and cold were also free; and the people demanded something more than liberty. The old watchwords still rang true; but they were not enough. And how to fill the void was the riddle that split the Liberal party. (1: 268–269)

This is a summation by a great historian — evidence of his powers of grand and visionary summations in a work otherwise including often particular and excessive details. Passages such as this will — and should — live and inspire historians as long as English history is written.

They surely lived long in his mind.* And now I must leap

---

* A stunning example. In 1887 Joseph Chamberlain wrote a conciliatory letter to Lord Randolph Churchill which included a Latin phrase: "Ira amantium redintegratio amoris" (loose translation: love between us will be stronger after our quarrel). More than forty years after

ahead and break the chronological sequence and say something about his *Marlborough,* written thirty years later: because that, too, had the purpose of vindicating an ancestor.

Marlborough consists of four volumes. The first volume was published in October 1933, the last in September 1938. These dates are telling. For Churchill wrote these very large volumes at the very time when he was deeply engaged in more than mundane politics, when he was the self-appointed Cassandra of the prospect of a coming second world war. Also: during those years he wrote and dictated more newspaper articles than perhaps ever before or after. And while working on the last two volumes of *Marlborough* he was also beginning to dictate the first chapters of his *History of the English-Speaking Peoples* (which he interrupted in 1939, returning to it well after the Second World War). What extraordinary energy! True: he was now able to gather and employ a considerable staff of historian amanuenses who brought documents to him, filled in gaps in his historical knowledge of a detail or even of a considerable period, the kind of assistance that other, less well-favored historians may justly envy: but the composition of the work, and its writing, were his own. We must compare Churchill's historianship not with that of professors (alas, there are such) whose research and other work is often the result of tasks they had farmed out to their graduate students. If there is any valid comparison at all, it must be with that of great artists such as Leonardo or Rubens or Rembrandt who,

---

Churchill had read and printed this letter (2: 347) he used the same phrase in a message to Franklin Roosevelt in 1945.

more than often, relied on groups of admiring painter-students to fill out details here and there, without compromising the genius of their master's grand design and of his craft. Maurice Ashley, who was one of Churchill's helpers in the work for *Marlborough*, wrote: "This gave me the opportunity to see Churchill at work as a historian, at a time when my heart was young, my mind malleable, and my memory good."*

Marlborough is Churchill's grandest, and strangest, work. Ashley thought that it was even better than *Lord Randolph Churchill*, which is debatable. More than any other of his works *Marlborough* could (and perhaps should) have been shortened. The four volumes (often published in two books, to which the following quotations refer) run more than two thousand pages.† The work is also — a word that I use with some reluctance — undisciplined. Its research was extraordinary. A great number of unpublished letters Churchill found in the muniment room of Blenheim (they are specially marked throughout the pages), but they are only a small part of all kinds of documents culled from a very large variety of archives and papers and books in England and throughout Europe. Yes, many of these were dug out and brought to Churchill by his assistants, but then *he* chose which to employ and how to employ them (sometimes exceedingly), and at what point. The footnotes are daunting. At one point (2: 673, note 1) Churchill evidently found it proper and necessary to illustrate one sentence in his

---

*Maurice Ashley, *Churchill as Historian*, New York, 1968, p. 4.

†Winston Churchill, *Marlborough: His Life and Times*, 2 vols., London, 1967.

text with a small numerical table, the fluctuating prices of wheat in England 1706 to 1714. But at another place (1: 116), writing about John Churchill's proposed marriage to the beautiful but not rich Sarah Jennings, Churchill wastes a page and a half on composing fictitious letters by the grooms' parents ("We may imagine some of them") objecting to the troth. Yet there are other excursions that are masterly (for example, an entire chapter, "The Europe of Charles II," which could be a model for historians). Others are unduly instructional: about fortresses, drills, musketry, and so on. I think that Churchill was also attracted to the history of Marlborough, his wars, his period, because they involved what to Churchill was and remained the inevitable connection between the destiny of England and the fate of Europe, or at least of Western Europe — whereto Marlborough and an English army had returned after an insular absence of nearly three hundred years.

Like in *Lord Randolph Churchill,* Churchill's magisterial depiction of the larger canvas, of the history of those times, succeeds better than his biographic vindication of his ancestor. Unlike in *Lord Randolph Churchill,* we may wonder why he undertook this herculean effort instead of a brief correction of the contemptuous rendering of Marlborough by Macaulay and other writers. We have seen that Churchill had a number of common traits with his father. With his ancestor John Churchill he had just about none. A great general Marlborough may have been. But he was also cold, calculating, frugal, secretive, avaricious — very much unlike his great descendant. (And, again unlike: "I do not like writing" 2: 581. One thing they had in common: their love for their wives.) By and large

Churchill, with all of his justifiable emphasis on the character and conditions of those times, fails to convince us that his ancestral hero was not a shrewd and crafty calculator in his contacts with the exiled James II (his once great benefactor whom he abandoned in 1688) and with James's illegitimate son Berwick (whose mother, Arabella, true, was a former mistress of James, and Marlborough's sister). There was also a crudeness in Marlborough's character when he, for instance, wrote to Queen Anne in 1710, forcing her to choose between her confidante, the plain Mrs. Masham (who had been intriguing against Sarah), and him. When the queen wrote a letter dismissing him (on New Year's Eve, 1711), he threw that into the fire. His answer to her the next day was not one of his best.

A very obvious mistake of *Marlborough* is Churchill's excessive and vindictive campaign against Macaulay — a strange and unusual exception to Churchill's usual magnanimity and to his willingness to forget past wrongs. But then the entire purpose of his *Marlborough* he set forth at the very beginning: "A long succession of the most famous writers of the English language have exhausted their resources of reproach and insult upon his name. Swift, Pope, Thackeray, and Macaulay in their different styles have vied with each other in presenting an odious portrait to posterity. Macpherson and Dalrymple have fed them with mis-leading and mendacious facts" (1: 17). Churchill's campaign against Macaulay goes on and on and on. About John Churchill's affair with the older, very rich, and influential Barbara Villiers: "How disgusting to pretend, with Lord Macaulay, a filthy, sordid motive for actions prompted by those overpowering conclusions which lead flaming from the crucible of life itself!" (1: 92) Once in awhile his research wonderfully succeeds: in a masterly footnote Churchill proves that in one instance Macaulay mistook William Penn for a minor writer by the name of Penne (1: 199). In sum: "It is beyond our hopes to overtake Lord Macaulay. The grandeur and sweep of his story-telling style carries him swiftly along. . . . We can only hope that Truth will follow swiftly enough to fasten the label 'Liar' to his genteel coat-tails" (1: 132). Macaulay was not the only historian who aroused Churchill's ire: about the Austro-German Onno Klopp: "A whine and drone of baffled spite arises from these wearisome, laborious chronicles" (1: 492).

Perhaps the sharpest criticism of *Marlborough* was made in 1934, after the publication of the first volume, in a small book by the Jacobite historian Malcolm V. Hay, *Winston Churchill and James II of England*. "Can Mr. Winston Churchill be trusted?" "Mr. Churchill, sweeping out of his way everything likely to impede the progress of his argument, has followed the technique not of history, but of fiction." In his conclusion Hay cites Churchill's own preface: "We await with meekness every correction or contradiction which the multiplicate knowledge of students and critics will supply" (1: 20). "If Mr. Churchill is really so willing to accept correction, he will apologize in his next volume for his unfairness to James II. Fairness often requires an effort, and a watchful supervision of will; it is here that Mr. Winston Churchill has failed."* Yes,

---

*Malcolm V. Hay, *Winston Churchill and James II of England*, London, 1936, pp. 8, 62.

Churchill believed that "the Jacobite records preserved in the
Scots College in Paris are one of the greatest frauds of history"
(1: 18–19). Yet he could be marvelously fair to evidences and
arguments contrary to his. "It is unfair to derive one's portrait
of [Queen] Anne from the writings of the Duchess of Marlborough" (whom Churchill unreservedly admired, 1: 166). That he
was not dogmatically anti-Catholic must appear from his ex-
quisite portrait of Pope Innocent XI (1: 229–230). And here is
a fine example of balance, credit given to the pro-Jacobite
James II of Hilaire Belloc: "A recent Catholic writer had por-
trayed the opposition to James as the resistance of the rich
and powerful. This is true. It was successful because the rich
and powerful championed the causes and prejudices which
the masses espoused, but without superior leadership were
unable to defend" (1: 217).

Finally, there are his splendid phrases and passages. Marlborough was supposed to have studied the Roman military
writer Vegetius in detail. "It has often been suggested that by
some occult dispensation our hero was able to extract various
modern sunbeams from this ancient cucumber" (1: 46). About
Harley's letters: "There is a personal awkwardness about them
and a scent of lamp-oil, redolent after two hundred years" (1:
540). "Scotland chewed the thongs of union morosely through
the misadventures of 1707" (2: 317). "An indifference to logic
where it is likely to lead to serious trouble is one of the strongest English characteristics" (1: 545).

Yet another book that Churchill published in the 1930s was
a collection of some of his pen portraits, with the title *Great
Contemporaries*. In its way this is one of his three biographical

works. Of course the craft of a biographer and that of a historian do not merely overlap, they are often the very same. And
Great Contemporaries was much more than a collection of dis-
parate pieces, and much much more than a potboiler. Many
of Churchill's portraits of various personalities (not all of them
British) are not only very well written but are marked with an
understanding that ranges beneath and beyond the art of portraiture.*

I turn now to Churchill's histories of the First and Second
World Wars. He wrote them in very different circumstances
and during very different chapters of his life — *The World Crisis*
in the 1920s, *The Second World War* between 1948 and 1953.
He worked during ten years on the first, during five on the
second. The first consists of five volumes, the second of six.
He had far more help from historians and assistants for the
second than for the first. Yet I am inclined to think that his
Second World War history is the better of the two. The great
military historian Sir Charles Oman was a severe critic of *The
World Crisis;* there were also others.† Churchill devotes too
many pages in it to justify some of his decisions, such as the
Dardanelles — though not without an admission of self-criti-
cism. Moreover, the quality of the successive volumes de-
creases. The last one, *The Eastern Front*, published in 1931 and
the shortest one, was almost an afterthought. (He wrote it

* Cf. his portrait of Hitler cited in Chapter 1.
† See also Robin Prior, *Churchill's World Crisis as History*, London,
1983.

when he was already deeply involved in his writing of *Marlborough*.) Again, the Defoe-inspired compound of history and autobiography works better in *The Second World War* than in his voluminous history of the First: but then this is natural, for he was the Prime Minister and the chief antagonist of Hitler's Germany through most of the Second. The quality and the consistency and the rhythm of the six volumes of *The Second World War* is steadier, more even than that of *The World Crisis*.

But there are grounds for criticism there, too. The most substantial criticism is apposite to its first volume, *The Gathering Storm*, in which — to mention but one example — his description of Stanley Baldwin is unbalanced and unfair. There are other such examples, though perhaps less self-justificatory than in *The World Crisis*. In *The Second World War* Churchill's main purpose is less to justify himself than to justify his perspective: if only the British and French governments had behaved better, this war could have been avoided. This is arguable. John Ramsden, not a customary critic of Churchill, in his valuable lecture cites Churchill who in *The Gathering Storm* insists that in 1936 Hitler could have been stopped, if only the French had mobilized: "There is no doubt that Hitler would have been compelled by his own General Staff to withdraw; and a check would have been given to his pretentions which might well have been fatal to his rule." "Note the way," Ramsden says, "in which that sentence slides imperceptibly from a confident 'there is no doubt' via two hopeful 'would have been[s]' to a suggestive 'might well have been.' It was on such a frail thread of syntax that hung Churchill's oft-repeated claim that (as he put it at Fulton), 'there never was a war in all history easier to prevent.'" This is very good.* On the other hand, there are many instances of Churchillian magnanimity in *The Second World War* — perhaps foremost among them his decision to omit entirely his struggle with Halifax, who wished to at least explore a potential negotiation with Hitler during five very critical days in May 1940. (Another example is the, earlier mentioned, toning down the record of his differences with the Americans in 1944–1945.) Plumb, otherwise very critical of Churchill's historianship, admits: "Churchill the historian lies at the very heart of the historiography of World War II, and will always remain there."†

There is yet another difference between the two world war histories. There is a purpose of *The Second World War* that is also extant in *A History of the English-Speaking Peoples*.‡ Both of them are exhortatory. I think it was Samuel Johnson who said that we are here less to instruct people than to remind them. In both of these, otherwise very different, multivolume works Churchill's purpose is to remind the English-speaking peoples of the world of their inheritance, of what they had been capable of achieving, of their very virtues. This is evident

---

* Ramsden, "That Will Depend on Who Writes the History," p. 14. Ramsden also notes that in February 1938 Churchill signed a letter of confidence, assuring Chamberlain of his support — contrary to the impression a reader receives from *The Gathering Storm*.

† Plumb, "The Historian," p. 166.

‡ Generally speaking, the last two volumes of *A History of the English-Speaking Peoples* are better than the first two. Churchill was not unduly interested in the Middle Ages.

from the "Moral" of *The Second World War:* "In War: Resolution. In Defeat: Defiance. In victory: Magnanimity. In Peace: Good Will" — but also in his decision not to write anything about those dramatic days and nights in late May 1940 where he prevailed, and when he was right and Halifax wrong. Instead, he writes that in those very days "the War Cabinet were all of one mind." And: "There was a white glow, overpowering, sublime, which ran through our island from end to end" (1: 89, 100).

"It must be admitted," Maurice Ashley says in the conclusion of his fine book *Churchill as Historian,* "that Churchill was wanting in that complete scientific application possible in university cloisters, though his powers of concentration and ability to master detail were terrific. . . . Churchill could be obstinate, as those who helped him write his books were aware, and though he might yield to persuasion, he was hard to persuade. This, I think it must be admitted, is Churchill's main weakness as a historical writer. Clio is a tough mistress and requires a lot of service. . . . He never had either the time or the inclination to absorb himself in it completely or to revise his work in detail in the light of later knowledge: he preferred to make history than to write it."* This is largely true (except perhaps the question whether "complete scientific application" is what historical reconstruction consists of, and whether it is really and truly practiced in university cloisters). It rings truer, and fairer, than David Reynolds's conclusion in his paper of the 2001 Churchill conference: "In the 1950s, one might

_____

* Ashley, *Churchill as Historian,* pp. 230–231.

say, Churchill was a prisoner of history — his own history of the 1930s. It proved easier to make history than to unmake it."* Reynolds exaggerates when he states that the accepted notions of Baldwin, Chamberlain, Munich, appeasement had been largely Churchill's work. Yet Reynolds deserves credit for his research in the Churchill papers in the Churchill Archives, his reconstructing much about how *The Gathering Storm* was written. John Ramsden, more sympathetic to Churchill, points out other shortcomings of Churchill's research, one as late as in 1948, when he had failed to have some of Franklin Roosevelt's letters released by President Truman.

But let me look, now, at a larger and deeper issue, going beyond and beneath Churchill's method and purpose in writing his histories (even as we ought to realize that purpose is often inherent in method, as every "why" in every "how"). In 1933 A. L. Rowse in *The End of an Epoch* declared that Churchill, "unlike Trotsky[!], has no philosophy of history." This was cited and repeated in 1962 by E. H. Carr in his *What Is History?*† This is absolute nonsense. These famous British academic intellectuals fail to see that Churchill had something far more essential than a systematic philosophy of history (about which the great historian Jacob Burckhardt had written that it is a contradiction in itself; "A philosophy of history is a centaur, a contradiction in terms: for history coordinates,

---

*Reynolds, "Churchill's Writing of History," p. 247.

†A. L. Rowse, *The End of an Epoch: Reflections on Contemporary History*, London, 1947, pp. 282–283; E. H. Carr, *What Is History?* New York, 1962, p. 54.

and hence is unphilosophical, while philosophy subordinates, and hence is unhistorical"). Churchill possessed something quite different: a historical philosophy. (Poor Trotsky! He *did* have a philosophy of history! It did him no good. I do not only mean his political career. His writings in exile show that his understanding of the historical realities of that time — the 1930s — were woefully wrong, the very opposite of Churchill's . . .) Thirty-five years and a Second World War later J. H. Plumb, in his essay about "The Historian," slips, slides (and falls) on another slippery slope, when he writes about Churchill's historianship: "There was, and is, in his work, a touch of the philistine." "He never mastered the giant intellectual figures of his youth and early middle age — Marx and Freud." (I am inclined to think that may have been to Churchill's advantage, not a handicap.) According to Plumb, omissions in *A History of the English-Speaking Peoples* are "indicative of Churchill's major fault both as a historian and as a statesman: he lacked a sense of the deeper motives that control society [Economics, Anyone?] and make it change, just as he lacked an interest in the deeper human motives [As, for example, in Hitler's?]."*

In 1962 E. H. Carr wrote: "Before you study the history, study the historian"; and "before you study the historian, study his historical and social environment." This half-truth† has been often applied to Churchill's historianship, wrongly. Ac-

---

*Plumb, "The Historian," pp. 142, 155.

†About this half-truth see John Lukacs, *At the End of An Age,* New Haven, 2002, pp. 68–69.

cording to Plumb, again, "To understand Churchill the historian, one must look closer at his inheritance, particularly the historical assumptions of his class." This is much too simple. As one of his most recent biographers, Roy Jenkins, writes: Churchill's aristocratic background was not "the key to his whole career. Churchill was far too many-faceted, idiosyncratic and unpredictable a character to allow himself to be imprisoned by circumstances of his birth."* Such different historians as Plumb and Charmley have categorized Churchill as a prototypical aristocratic Whig, which is debatable from his historical judgments alone (examples of which are his treatments of the Whigs of the 1680s in *Marlborough* and those of two centuries later in *Lord Randolph Churchill*).

Yet Plumb, who asserts the insufficiency of Churchill's extensive research for *Marlborough,* writes: "Although open to criticism as history, it remains a splendid work of literary art." And about *A History of the English-Speaking Peoples:* "It contains his secular faith. As history, it fails, hopelessly fails; as a monument of a great Englishman's sense of the past, it is a brilliant success." But are those two matters entirely separable? If you have the right (and fine) sense of the past, can your history be entirely wrong? After all, Plumb also writes that "history was not, for Churchill, like painting, something one turned to for relaxation or merely to turn an honest guinea to meet his mountainous expenses. History was the heart of his faith; it permeated everything which he touched, and it was the mainspring of his politics and the secret of his immense

* Roy Jenkins, *Churchill,* New York, 2001, p. 3.

mastery." "And I venture to think that only a statesman steeped in history could have roused and strengthened the nation in the way Churchill did during those years." As Maurice Ashley concludes about Churchill's historicism: "It is to his credit that he valued the verdicts of history and that he was conscious in all he did and said as Prime Minister that historians would one day examine and judge him."* These are proper tributes to Churchill the maker of history, to a statesman whose mind was steeped in history. Yet I think that another tribute may still be due: to Churchill the historical writer. There exist bad histories that are written tellingly or even well; but there can be no good history that is not told or written well. After all, whatever the research, there is no historical fact the meaning of which exists separately from its statement, from its very phrasing.

Churchill formed his own style. He was influenced by Gibbon and Macaulay but he did not emulate them. Stunning passages and phrases are abundant in every one of his books. I reproduce but a few of them, collected and jotted down on various scraps of paper in a near-lifetime of reading. In *Lord Randolph Churchill* about the Whigs: "The debate was heralded for several days by much parliamentary snarling." About some of the Tories: "the prosaic authoritarians who chafe the hearts of Celtic peoples." In *Marlborough* about Charles II: "Manoeuvre, fence, and palter as he might, he always submitted, and always meant to submit, with expedition to the deep growl

---

*Plumb, "The Historian," pp. 142, 134, 151, 153, 155, 137, 167; Ashley, *Churchill as Historian*, p. 231.

of his subjects and to the authority of their inexpugnable institutions." About James II in 1686: "Nay, he would not reject even the dim, stubborn masses who had swarmed to Monmouth's standards in the West, or had awaited him elsewhere, whose faith was the very antithesis of his own, and whose fathers had cut off his father's head." In *The World Crisis* about 1914: Germany "clanked obstinately, recklessly, awkwardly towards the crater and dragged us all with her." And of 28 July 1914, the First Fleet leaving Portsmouth for Scapa Flow, through the English Channel: "scores of gigantic castles of steel wending their way across the misty, shining sea, like giants bowed in anxious thought." An immortal passage! Or about the German admiral, von Spee, cut off from refueling or repairing his ships: "He was a cut flower in a vase, fair to see, yet bound to die and die very soon if the water was not renewed." About a general who ordered the evacuation from Gallipoli: "He came, he saw, he capitulated." In *The Aftermath* about Russia after the Bolshevik revolution: "Russia has been frozen in an indefinite winter of sub-human doctrine and superhuman tyranny." In *A History of the English-Speaking Peoples* about King Charles, sequestrated in Carisbrooke Castle, 1647: "Here, where a donkey treads an endless water-wheel, he dwelt for almost a year, defenceless, sacrosanct, a spiritual King, a coveted tool, an intriguing parcel, an ultimate sacrifice." (That solitary sad little donkey going round and round the waterwheel captured Churchill's imagination. He must have felt that he had to put it into his description. This was not the employment of a well-known historical cliché, not like the Capitoline geese or a kingdom for a horse: I know only of one history of Charles II or the English civil war where that donkey has been recorded.)

Churchill's historical philosophy was evident. He did not only ponder history deeply, by which I mean its events and its course. What he wrote or said on occasion about the very nature of historical knowledge are worth citing, for many reasons, one of them being that they have stood the test of time. In *Lord Randolph Churchill:* "There is scarcely any more abundant source of error in history than the natural desire of writers — regardless of the overlapping and inter-play of memories, principles, prejudices and hopes, and the reaction of physical conditions — to discover or provide simple explanations for the actions of their characters." Or consider this passage about the Home Rule debates — echoing Burke, who said that one cannot and should not perceive men entirely separate from their historic circumstances: "A generation may arise in England who will question [their] policy . . . as little as we question the propriety of Catholic Emancipation and who will study the records of the fierce disputes of 1886 with the superior manner of a modern professor examining the controversies of the early Church. But that will not prove the men of 1886 wrong or foolish in speech and action." (Well — some of them were . . .) Or this great passage from his funeral oration for Chamberlain in November 1940: "It is not given to human beings, happily for them, to foresee or to predict to any large extent the unfolding course of events. . . . [But later] there is a new proportion, there is another scale of values. History with its flickering lamp stumbles along the trail of the past, trying to reconstruct its scenes, to revive its echoes, and kindle with pale gleams the passions of former days."

"The meanest historian owes something to truth."*

"Churchill the Historian" is a book yet to be written.†

---

* Churchill (in 1899!), cited by Ashley, *Churchill as Historian*, p. 47.

† Frederick Woods, *A Bibliography of the Works of Sir Winston Churchill* (2 rev. ed.), London, 1975. An extensive bibliography, prepared by Ronald I. Cohen (Manotick, Ontario), is to be published soon. Cf. also Eric Stainbaugh, *Winston Churchill, a Reference Guide*, Boston, 1985.

7

His failures. His critics.

Churchill: A Study in Failure, 1900–1939, is the title of a work by Robert Rhodes James, written and published more than thirty years ago. It is one of the best (I am inclined to rank it at least among the half-dozen best) books written about Churchill, of which many hundreds exist. It is melancholy to record that its author died in the prime of his life. He may have enriched us with more good books, perhaps yet another about Churchill's life after 1939. But 1 September 1939 (or, latest, 10 May 1940) is the main caesura. Before that Churchill's errors, mistakes, misfortunes were numerous enough for many responsible people to distrust him, indeed to attribute them to failures of his character. Still he came to be the Prime Minister of Britain, and thereafter the savior of Western civilization in *his* finest hour. In the short run his assumption of the premiership may have been predictable at that time, since the accumulation of his warnings about Hitler had come true. In the long run of retrospect not at all: it was a miracle of sorts. Or, to cite my favorite proverb: "God writes straight with crooked lines."

And crooked lines they were, because of his many misfortunes, many of them of his own making. He had an extraordinarily quick mind, something that may be a tremendous
asset — at times — but also something that may lead to premature conclusions, not to speak of the expectable reactions of
people bereft of such mental acuity and agility, their reactions
ranging from reserve and caution to distrust and envy. In this
short book, and in this short chapter, I can but list, or sum
up, his mistakes and failures. Some of them are well known.
Others are not. Well known is his unprecedented, and most
unusual, moving from one of the great parliamentary parties
to the other, and then back again. He started his political and
parliamentary career as a Conservative in 1900, but he was no
party stalwart but rather a rebel; then he switched to the Liberals but became disappointed with that party too; after twenty
years he rejoined the Conservatives, but, again, he was a rebel
in their ranks. He knew what that meant. "The Conservatives
never liked me," he once said — more accurately, most of them
did not — indeed, not until July 1940 did they become ranged,
more or less solidly, behind him.

Yet leading politicians often recognized the talents of this
maverick, despite some of the disputatious and colorful incidents in his early career. Thus he was elevated to Home Secretary and then in 1911 to First Lord of the Admiralty. With the
prospect of a potential war with Germany, to be fought on the
high seas between enormous fleets, this was perhaps the most
important governmental post before the war. Yet Churchill's
training and his experiences had been military; he knew little

about the navy when he assumed his post. His performance as First Lord was controversial. Historians are still debating its pros and cons, nearly a century later. His best achievement was the readiness of the Home Fleet in July 1914, a state for which he deserved to be credited (he himself declared that this was one of the most important achievements of his life). At the same time he was injudicious and impulsive, often with disastrous or at least near-disastrous results. James cites a "most injudicious speech [Churchill] delivered at Liverpool on 21 September 1914, in which he declared that if the German Navy did not come out to fight 'it would be dug out like rats from a hole.'" Next day three British cruisers were sunk, an event that occasioned the King to remark to the Prime Minister, Asquith, that "the rats came out of their own accord and to our cost."* A fortnight later Churchill made a dramatic announcement: he would lead a British force to Antwerp, to save that important port from German occupation: if necessary, he would resign his Admiralty in exchange for such a command. He did not need resign; he got his command, but the expedition failed.

Now we come to the Dardanelles. Very early in the war, earlier than others (including Kitchener), Churchill saw the promiseless, indeed, the horrid prospect of static war on the Western Front, mass armies mired in mud and barbed wire. His imaginative mind, strengthened by his knowledge of ex-

---

* Robert Rhodes James, *Churchill: A Study in Failure, 1900–1939,* New York, 1970, p. 66.

amples from earlier histories of British endeavors in the Mediterranean, led to the idea of a great naval task force thrusting through the strait of the Dardanelles, and then reaching Constantinople in a day or two, thus knocking Turkey (which seemed Germany's weakest ally) instantly out of the war: a dramatic triumph which would also lead to the opening of a grand seagate to Russia as well as to a rapidly coalescing Balkan front of states, endangering Germany's major ally the Austrian empire from the south. In late October 1914 Churchill had brought Lord Fisher back to the Admiralty: First Sea Lord. "Jacky" Fisher had the elements of genius, including many kinds of foresight, accorded to some of the greatest English admirals since Nelson. He was now over seventy, but his mental agility (sometimes with its odd outpourings) was extraordinary. He and Churchill had much in common. Each admired the other's quickness of mind. But Fisher thought (and said) that the Dardanelles plan was wrong because unachievable. Still, Churchill succeeded in pushing his plan through. Fisher was right. Battleships and other warships were sunk; the rest of the fleets had to turn around; their naval artillery could not (and should not have been expected to) destroy the guns of the fortifications on land; the subsequent decision to land troops and conquer the Gallipoli peninsula over land turned into another sad disaster. Churchill was wrong—not only tactically but also strategically. What we know of the ability and the mobility of the Germans strongly suggests that even if the thrust through the Dardanelles had succeeded, even if Constantinople and Turkey had been thrust out of the war, a consequent advance through the Balkans was not the way to get at the vitals of Germany.*

Fisher resigned, and Churchill had to go. It was the bleakest time of his career. Years later, writing his history of the Great War, he defended himself, without bitterness or vindictiveness, giving us the impression that with a bit more luck (and intelligence) the ships could have gone through: but, as I have said, the worth of the entire plan was arguable. Yet there was one, seldom remarked, Churchillian argument in *The World Crisis* that calls for attention. At the end of his hundreds of pages devoted to the Dardanelles and Gallipoli, he wrote that the failure of the effort there was a fatal contribution to the Russians' disappointment with their Western allies, to their unwillingness to go on with the war, to the eventual revolution and collapse of Russia. A cogent and convincing argument. (Except for Churchill's belief that the promised delivery of Constantinople to Russia, a glittering prize, was worth the game: and how long would *that* have lasted, in an age of nationalisms?)

---

*With all respect due to Fisher, much of the same applied to his own audacious plan, his alternative to the Dardanelles as well as to the stalemate in Flanders and France. Fisher proposed to send the Home Fleet into German waters, blocking the Kiel Canal and then sailing around Denmark into the Baltic, landing on the flat beaches of Pomerania, less than ninety miles from Berlin, putting ashore British and more than one hundred thousand Russian troops. A plan probably doomed to failure, just as was the British landing in Holland with British and Russian troops in 1799.

In any event—this Churchillian perspective suggests the connection with the next failure in his career, his insistent propagation of fighting the Bolsheviks, of at least a partial British involvement in the Russian civil war. Three, at most four years after the Dardanelles we see him arguing, against Lloyd George, against his government, against Britain's military chiefs, against the majority of the British people, trying to topple the Bolshevik regime in Russia, principally (though not exclusively) by furnishing and arming and otherwise assisting White generals, perhaps especially General Denikin, struggling against the Reds, marching up and down the Russias. And here Churchill failed too, less because of his inability to impress his government than because of the fatal weaknesses of the Russian Whites themselves. "Antwerp, the Dardanelles, Denikin," Winston Churchill was bad news: thus his enemy Sir Henry Wilson in 1919.

He recovered. His political career was not over. He was included in Cabinets: Minister of Munitions, War and Air Minister,* Colonial Office. In 1924 he switched parties again: he had, at best, a lukewarm welcome within the Conservative Party. But an outcast he was not; there were leaders who thought that they had to take into account his unusual capacities. So in 1925 there came to him another high office, the Chancellor-

---

* During 1919 and 1921 Churchill drastically reduced the then ambitious plans of the air staff by at least 80 percent. (It may be interesting to note that his father, otherwise a fairly militant nationalist, had tried to reduce the army and navy allocations twenty-five years earlier when he was Chancellor of the Exchequer, leading to his resignation from the Salisbury cabinet.)

ship of the Exchequer. And there developed another failure. In 1911 he knew very little about naval affairs when he became the head of the Admiralty; in 1925 he knew even less about economics and finance when he became the head of the treasury. Unlike in 1911, when he was enthusiastic in his learning and interest in the navy, in 1925 he was (and remained) unenthusiastic and not very interested in the theories and the jargon of economists. Yet the subsequent failure was not necessarily of his own making. He relied on competent advice when restoring the British pound to the gold standard of prewar. It was not because of his incompetent handling of that business that it failed to work.

Except among certain Conservatives his reputation did not suffer much from this stint. He went on, making his way in the world, including the United States, by more and more lectures, journalism, writing and publication of his histories of the First World War; his readership was large. And he was still an imperialist — at a time when some Englishmen consciously, and many others less consciously, had grown weary of Empire, or at least of the strictness of their imperial responsibilities. The result was yet another public sally, a great protest, a failure. It went on for years. He attacked the governments' (first Conservative, then Labour, then National) decision to grant Dominion status to India. His declarations and speeches and articles sounded often extreme (even though his prophecies ought not be easily dismissed). They are well known by historians, there is no need (and no place) to illustrate them with excerpts. I must, however, cite Robert Rhodes James's summary judgment: "When, today, people wonder why Churchill was not regarded seriously by so many politicians and journalists at this time, his [irresponsible] performances [of that time] should be remembered. What may be forgiven in a young politician seeking to make his name and attract attention — however irresponsible — is not easily forgiven to a senior ex-Cabinet minister on a matter of such considerable importance."* He had passed sixty, he had entered the seventh decade of his life when the India Bill was finally passed in 1935; he was disregarded by his own party, dismissed from the minds of many, a perhaps interesting but marginal figure at best.

He was a reactionary, rather than a conservative, on the edge of the spectrum of British politics. He was agitated by the issue of India during nearly six years; but there was another preoccupation of his mind around 1930, a disillusionment with liberal and parliamentary democracy, with its corroding institutions, with its prospects. One, but only one, example of this was his respect and even admiration for Mussolini, whom he met in 1927. "A really great man," he stated in 1935, praising him as late as 1937, though changing his mind about him a year later. Churchill had a certain appreciation for authoritarian rulers, which is how he saw Mussolini: a strong restorer of law and order, scotching the danger of Communism, and governing within the limits of civilization, maintaining many of its freedoms. He was not altogether wrong in seeing the difference between authoritarianism and totalitarian tyranny (even though it was Mussolini who may have been first to em-

---

*James, *Churchill,* p. 234.

ploy the word *totalitarian,* positively, as early as 1926). Another example: in 1931, contributing the preface to a book entitled *Dictatorship* by an Austrian (Otto Forst de Battaglia), Churchill wrote that under certain conditions a dictatorial regime may be timely, though of course not for Britain. In his splendidly written memoir, *My Early Life,* in 1930 he looked back at the political scene in 1900. "I must explain that in those easy days we had a real political democracy led by a hierarchy of states- men, and not a fluid mass distracted by newspapers. . . . All this was before the liquefaction of the British political system had set in." That same year, in his Romanes lecture (but also on other occasions), he questioned the principle and the prac- tice of universal suffrage. "Democracy has shown itself care- less about those very institutions by which its own political status has been achieved. It seems ready to yield up the tangi- ble rights hard won in rugged centuries to party organizations, to leagues and societies, to military chiefs or to dictatorships in various forms." About universal suffrage he wrote in 1932: "Why at this moment should we force upon the untutored races of India that very system, the inconveniences of which are now felt even in the most highly developed nations, the United States, Germany, France and in England itself?"*

He clearly preferred Fascism to Communism. As late as in 1937 he even said in Parliament: "I will not pretend that if I had to choose between Communism and Nazi-ism, I would choose Communism." This must not be misunderstood. I

---

*Cited by Robert Rhodes James in "The Politician," *Churchill Re- vised: A Critical Assessment,* New York, 1969, pp. 113–114.

think that he regarded Communism as A Lie, and National Socialism as A Half-Truth; and he knew (as had such different sages as St. Thomas Aquinas and La Rochefoucauld) that a half-truth is more dangerous because more attractive than a lie. That at the same time, 1937, he saw Hitler's Third Reich being (and fast becoming) more dangerous than the Soviet Union we know. But, at least in this writer's opinion, we must give him credit for something else, too. He, on the extreme right of the Conservatives, would have had ample reasons to sympathize with Hitler. The "Tory Democracy," which his father and he himself espoused, had after all some things in common with the concordance between nationalism and socialism that Hitler espoused and which seemed to be a worldwide development, albeit in different forms, in the 1930s. Across the world, and even in Britain, many a right-wing Conservative, and also many a right-wing Labourite (consider only Mosley) not only chose to give Hitler the benefit of doubt but came close to sympathizing with his cause. Churchill did not so choose — because of his vision, and because of his character.

He was also a man who could, and would, change his mind, and not because of opportunism. He who had questioned universal suffrage (as late as 1935 he thought that perhaps it ought to be either limited, or doubled to heads of households) became the champion of and world spokesman for parliamentary democracy during the war. (So did he change his mind about Irish Home Rule and about female suffrage decades earlier. In his biography of his father he cited him: "An unchanging mind is an admirable possession — a possession which I de-

voutly hope I shall never possess.") As late as 1935 he spoke
of "those faded flowers of Victorian Liberalism."* But there
was now another, greater preoccupation in his mind: Germany
Rising. To paraphrase his words about what had suddenly occurred in July 1914: the dustclouds and torpid mists of India
faded back, and a strange light began immediately, and by perceptible gradations, to fall and grow upon the map of Europe.
He was almost alone to see it that way. Most of his contemporaries did not. We know this now. But we also know that he
was wrong in his exaggerated figures of German armaments,
especially of the German air force. He, who had been an early
and very reasonable advocate of tank warfare in 1917, was also
wrong about the approaching prospect of armored motorized
offensives. He was wrong, too, about the vulnerability of warships from the air. Yet these were not the reasons of his failure
to impress Parliament at that time, including members who,
while not necessarily agreeing with him, had been often interested or at least amused by his rhetoric. In the years 1934 to
1938 they thought that he was unduly repetitious. He was beginning to bore them. Then to these shortcomings came added,
substantially, his bullheaded advocacy of Edward VIII during
the abdication crisis in 1936; as A. J. P. Taylor writes: "He made
every possible blunder during the crisis."† On one occasion
he was shouted down in the Commons; as Geoffrey Best writes:
"It was the most humiliating event in his parliamentary career."

*_Lord Randolph Churchill_, London, 1906, 1: 341.
†A. J. P. Taylor _English History, 1914–1945_, Oxford, 1965, p. 404.

In January 1938 he assailed the Irish Treaty, even though that was a fairly reasonable one.

Thus we come to the year 1938, which was perhaps the nadir of his political career, while it was Hitler's best year. Churchill was now clearly the adversary of Neville Chamberlain (who as early as 1925 had expressed his dislike of Churchill). Their temperaments were very different. In 1938 so were their policies, and the course they attempted to set for their nation. Britain should not be involved in a European war in order to oppose Hitler, Chamberlain thought (and said), while Churchill said: if must, we must. In retrospect, Churchill seems to have been right; in his own retrospect he wrote and insisted upon that ten years later, in the first volume of his history of the Second World War. Yet he was wrong — at least in one sense, even though he did not admit this. I argued in an earlier chapter that contrary to his belief in 1938, and also contrary to his postwar reconstruction, there is little evidence and no reason to believe that Stalin's Russia would have stood on the side of the Western democracies in a military support of Czechoslovakia in October 1938. More important — though perhaps also more arguable — is the consideration, resting on substantial evidence, that had there been a quick war over Czechoslovakia in 1938, Hitler would have won it, because France and Britain, their armies as well as their public opinion, even less prepared than they were to be a year later, would have either been inclined or forced to accept accomplished facts. Yes: Churchill's attack on the Munich "settlement" and on the Chamberlain government was one of his greatest speeches; yet while he was morally right, he may also have been practically wrong.

All of this was redeemed in Nineteen-Forty.

That we know — or ought to know. Still we must recognize — or at least, list — his failures during the war, by which I mean military moves or strategic ideas that were mostly due to his insistence. There was the dreary failure of the Norwegian campaign in 1940, which was largely the result of his planning (but, again, crooked lines turning straight — the Norway debacle led to his premiership). Other instances of his mistaken judgments included Dakar, the disaster of the two capital ships in the Sea of Malay, Singapore, Anzio. Of course it is neither reasonable nor possible to ascribe all of these failures to Churchill's war leadership — that is, to his planning. Their actual execution was often wanting. There remains another, larger, issue. We have seen that until mid-1943 he was able to impress and influence the Americans about overall strategy in Europe. He was still able to make them agree, at least to some extent, to his peripheral strategy, to thrust, after the liberation of North Africa, into what he called "the soft underbelly" of Europe, through the Mediterranean. Yes, a soft underbelly that was — but after Sicily and Naples the advance of the Anglo-American armies in Italy became an often desperately slow, upward crawl. And after the Apennines would come the Alps, and their superbly capable German defenders. There are military historians who have written that the entire Italian campaign may have been unneeded; and others, that the great invasion of Western Europe could and should have been mounted in 1943, not in 1944, with incalculable results, also ending the war sooner. That we will never know.

What we know is that near the end of the war Churchill was

often (but not always) tired; that he had suffered illnesses in 1943 and 1944, though far from incapacitating ones, as was the case with Roosevelt. There were a few instances — though there were many instances to the contrary — when his mental quickness was insufficient compensation for not having done his homework. Such was his behavior during the conference at Potsdam. But there was something more important: his failure to convince the Americans, to have his way with them, in 1944–1945 as well as in 1952–1954, as we have already seen. This had much to do with an inclination that sometimes worked in his favor but sometimes did not. It was the inclination of a man who was the votary of the written word. He would marshal and arrange and list and phrase his arguments clearly and all-includingly, and then send them off with a sense of relief, as if they had now been said and done: but though written and said they always were, done at times they were not. In 1940 ("Action This Day") this often worked; in 1944–1945 and later it often did not. His failure to convince Americans was perhaps the only great failure in the later years of a great career.

There were failures in that career that could hardly have been avoided. There were others for which Churchill was responsible. Here we come to a biographer's question — which, however, cannot be restricted, as if a biographer's work were one thing, and a historian's another. What were the shortcomings of his character? After all, that is what biographers attribute to their subjects. Yet this book is not a biographical or psychic analysis but a historical essay. Consequently the great divide of 1940 matters again. So many men and women did not like or trust him before that year. Half a book may not be enough to list them and their condemnations of Churchill. They were accumulating — understandably enough — early in his career. *The Spectator* in 1911, at the occasion of his appointment to First Lord: "He has not the loyalty, the dignity, the steadfastness and the good sense which makes an efficient head of a great office." *The National Review* called him a mountebank, a windbag, a political gambler. Even people who otherwise liked him, for example, A. G. Gardner, editor of *The Daily News,* in 1908: "To the insatiable curiosity and the enthusiasm of a child he joins the frankness of the child. He has no reserves and no shams. He has that scorn of concealment that belongs to a caste which never doubts itself." A fair assessment; but perhaps more typical was Queen Alexandra after the Dardanelles: "all that stupid, foolhardy Winston Churchill's fault." Foolhardy he may have been; stupid not. The assessment by his enemy Bonar Law, in 1917, was echoed by many others throughout Churchill's life: "I think he has very unusual intellectual ability, but at the same time he seems to have an entirely unbalanced mind." (Twenty-three years later we may find nearly identical phrases, word by word, in Halifax's diary and letters.) Churchill's brashness, his impetuosity, his rhetoric (the language rather than the delivery: contrary to the accepted view he was no natural orator; there were imperfections in his pronunciation; he knew that, hence he rehearsed his speeches privately often), his changes of parties and of positions, his journalism, "his lifelong weakness for bounders."* These judgments did not suddenly disappear

---

* An important point. See Roy Jenkins, *Churchill,* New York, 2001, p. 299.

when he got the Prime Ministership in May 1940. But then something happened that, in a way, had been foretold by a young woman he had liked early in his life: "The first time you meet Winston you see all his faults, and the rest of your life you spend in discovering his virtues." Thus the people of Britain (including not a few of his former adversaries and critics) in 1940 and after.

Of course a man's character does not change much, if at all, surely not after the sixty-fifth year of his life. His impetuosity, the rapid dartings of his mind went on to prevail. They disconcerted some of his military advisers who thought and said that Churchill's ideas were too many, and among the many most of them impractical: a typical critic was Lord Alanbrooke, with evidence in his various published diaries. But they were a minority: by and large Churchill's reputation, an appreciation of his historical role, after 1940 has been overwhelming. However, there were — and are — exceptions: people who were indifferent or uninterested in his career before 1940 but who expressed their dislike of his leadership or of his rhetoric or even of his entire perspective of the war. Such were military historians like General J. F. C. Fuller;* writers and public figures such as Evelyn Waugh and Malcolm Muggeridge and Alan Clark; historians such as David Reynolds and Sheila Lawlor (at least to some extent); John Charmley (to whose work I must return); among American populist and right-wing Republi-

---

* It should be noted that this able man had been a supporter of Oswald Mosley, and a respectful admirer of Hitler's Germany as late as September 1939.

can figures such as Patrick Buchanan whose arguments and phrases concerning Churchill occasionally reveal something like a deep-seated contempt (as do all the works of David Irving). Two matters are latent here. One – the minor one – is the expectable, and even predictable, development of historical perspectives. After all, we are in the twenty-first century now, more than sixty years after 1940, and nearly a half-century after Churchill's death. The general and often near-universal appreciation of certain men and of certain events is eventually followed by their revision and correction, at times because of the new discovery of documents and of their evidence but mostly because of changing perspectives – after which second phase another, again slightly different phase may follow. But history – our knowledge and our understanding of it – is not like a pendulum. It is not mechanical or automatic: it does not swing back, certainly not to where it was. We are – at least in this writer's opinion – living at a time when another, major matter ought to be considered, some symptoms of which, consciously or not, may be detected in the writings of certain historians but also in the utterances of a few public figures. Directly, or indirectly, they all concern Churchill's place in the history of Britain and also in that of the twentieth century at large.

The matter is Britain's situation – and her destiny – between America and Germany. I wrote earlier that Britain's leaders made their fateful choice of allying with their ancient enemy France in 1904 with the background knowledge that this choice had been made easier by knowing that American enmity to Britain no longer existed. This realization accorded with Churchill's convictions. We have seen that there were times when he expected little from Americans and when he was quite critical of them. But in the large course of events this did not much matter, and by 1940 the choice was stark and clear: increasing dependence on the United States (and the eventual abandonment of at least some of the Empire) was desirable, perhaps even unavoidable: an accord with Germany (even with the preservation of the Empire) absolutely not. Few people, certainly in Britain, had doubts about that choice; few have them now. We have seen that Churchill had his troubles with the Americans; but then his emphatic proposition of a special relationship between Britain and the United States has remained current, accepted by a variety of British and American leaders, no matter how slight its actual applications were (and are). Yet lately there have been some signs of rethinking. The historian Niall Fergusson wrote, as we have seen, that Britain may have been wrong in entering the First World War, that a more or less united Europe, largely under German leadership, could have been acceptable and even propitious for Britain in the long run. John Charmley has gone so far as to say that even during the Second World War, Churchill should have considered an accord with Hitler. Often it is not difficult to detect inclinations of anti-Americanism beneath such arguments. At the beginning of the twenty-first century their appearance may be significant, though not — yet — important. They are greatly overshadowed by the British debate of a different dilemma, whether to join "Europe" or not. Still, it is possible that in the twenty-first century, unlike in the twentieth, Britain and America may be drifting apart. Intelligent people must, sooner or later, consider a closer political and military (more than economic and bureaucratic) British association with Europe, including Germany, together with a receding British dependence on the United States.

Yet the admiration of Churchill among Americans is, at least at this time of writing, perhaps higher and more general than ever before. Not in Germany, however. Many serious German historians of the Second World War have attributed to Churchill a rigid and single-minded hatred of Germany, an obsession to conquer and destroy it, come what may.* Echoes of such a portraiture of Churchill have surfaced, on occasion,

* Examples: Andreas Hillgruber: Hitler's offers to Britain were "seriously meant" and "subjectively, honest," in *Hitlers Strategie* (1965), p. 144, note 1, but also throughout Hillgruber's other works: Churchill's desire was to destroy Prussia and Germany. The naval historian Karl Klee: Churchill "did not foresee that [his] policy would only lead to the replacement of a strong Germany by the overwhelming power of Russia." The diplomatic historian Martin Bernd: "Churchill's real motive for taking up the fight against Hitler-Germany and his final political aim are still controversial. Winston Churchill did not understand Germany and German culture in general, let alone National Socialism in particular. . . . Maybe he was guided, at least partly, by his personal ambitions not only to write history but to shape it. . . . Although the glory of Britain and Churchill ended in 1945, the myths about Churchill and his time will linger on in a world much more out of order than Britain seems to have been in its 'finest hour.' " In "Churchill and Hitler, 1940: Peace or War?" Bernd's article in R. A. C. Parker, ed., *Winston Churchill: Studies in Statesmanship,* London, 1995, p. 96. Note that (1) every one of the above sentences is highly questionable; (2) throughout his article Bernd relies on Charmley; (3) this was written *not* by a German right-wing historian!

even in estimable German newspapers, such as the *Frankfurter Allgemeine*. Austria's potential Chancellor, Jörg Haider, called Churchill "a war criminal" in one of his recent speeches — presumably thinking of the heavy British bombing of German cities during the war (though not of the fact that Churchill had been primarily instrumental in 1943 in convincing both Roosevelt and Stalin to declare the independence of Austria as one of their joint war aims). Of course, there were many instances of Churchill's harsh opinions and advocacies of warfare against Germany. He was also wrong in often attributing German aggressiveness and brutality to Prussianism,* overlooking the peculiarly Bavarian (and Austrian-German) element in National Socialism and Hitler. Perhaps the most questionable instance of his Germanophobe inclinations was his lack of interest in, indeed his dismissal of, the German — many of them aristocratic, and Prussian — conspirators who attempted to kill Hitler and overthrow his criminal regime in July 1944. (At least one important factor in Churchill's reactions at that time was his concern lest Germans — and there were accumulating evidences of such intentions at that very time — attempt to separate and sow trouble between the British-Americans and the Russians.) Yet it was neither opportunism nor calculation but his natural generosity that changed his mind (and heart) about Germany soon after 1918 and immediately after May 1945. Besides, as he wrote in the early 1930s: "I have always laid down the doctrine that the redress of the just

---

* Churchill's dislike of "Prussianism" emerged during and after his visit to Berlin in 1909.

grievance of the vanquished should precede the disarmament of the victors. Little was done to redress the grievances of the Treaties of Versailles and Trianon." In 1945 Konrad Adenauer, the future postwar chancellor of Germany, was supposed to have said of Churchill: "a hater of Germans," but three years later: "a man of vision." Still: many Germans have not, even now, come to terms with Churchill's place in history, as also many of them (though in different ways) have not yet come to terms with Hitler's.

I wrote about Churchill's visionary qualities in the first chapter of this little book; but neither was his great adversary Hitler devoid of foresight. On 6 November 1938 he spoke: "I naturally cannot prevent the possibility of this gentleman entering the [British] government in a couple of years [which is what happened] but I can assure you that I will prevent him from destroying Germany [which did not happen]." He despised Churchill, describing him often as a drunkard, behind whom stood "the Jews." Of course Churchill was neither a teetotaler nor a Judaeophobe. But he understood Hitler better than Hitler understood him, what Hitler might or might not do. Together with the qualities of his leadership and his courage, this was why Churchill did not lose the war in 1940. Six years later, in 1946, he was right again in his warning against Russia's iron curtain.*

* At that very moment both Churchill and George Kennan expressed views that were far from popular or accepted. Kennan found it necessary to emphasize the dangers of aggressive and expansive Communism; Churchill the dangers of a rigidly congealing division of Europe. Soon afterward Kennan himself became disillusioned with the ideo-

"His failures. His critics." Near the end of this chapter I must attempt a critical analysis of the work of a British historian, whose purpose has been to revise the accepted view of Churchill and of the Second World War. John Charmley's *Churchill: The End of Glory: A Political Biography* (1993) was prototypical, for most of his subsequent writings repeated his thesis in this large work: Churchill had talents, but his faults were enormous, leading to the end not only of the British Empire but of British power. Going to war with Hitler's Germany in 1939 was wrong; so was the refusal to make peace with Hitler in 1940 and again in 1941, when Hitler attacked Russia; the alliance with Russia during the war was wrong; and the worst mistake was Churchill's "most servile grovelling to the Americans," whom he "may have seen as a branch of the English-speaking Peoples but they were, in fact, foreigners who disliked the British Empire even more than did Hitler." Roosevelt was a combination of Uriah Heep and Machiavelli, "a healthy distrust of all things British . . . was part of the mental luggage of any good New Dealer." "One simple fact: the Prime Minister's policy in 1940 had, in effect, failed. Far from securing Britain's independence, it had mortgaged it to America."

Well, the mental luggage of the New Dealers, including American help to Britain against Hitler's Germany, had many motives and purposes, but that of mortgaging Britain was not among them. But then Charmley's interpretation of Chur-

---

logication and militarization of successive American governments. (It is pleasant to record that at the time of this writing the reputation of both of them remains high.)

chill's relationship to America issues from his interpretation
of the entire Second World War. According to Charmley,
Churchill was wrong when he said that to "allow Germany to
dominate Europe was contrary to the whole of our history."
Churchill was a warmonger, while Chamberlain was right:
"Chamberlain was planning for the future, Churchill for Ar-
mageddon." "Britain had gone to war in 1939 in a spasm of
self-righteous indignation, convinced that as a Great Power it
was her duty to defeat Nazi Germany." Both before and after
the fall of France and before the Battle of Britain, "in the eyes
of many sensible folk, the time had come to think about coming to terms with Hitler." When Hitler invaded Russia, there
was another supreme "opportunity that Churchill let slip."
Thereafter Churchill "helped to raise the spectre of a menace
which was even greater than the one he had destroyed." Leaving aside the question whether a peace settlement with a victorious Hitler was at all possible, let alone desirable or enduring,
Charmley does not see, or wish to see, what Churchill saw
early in the war (and what I phrased earlier): either all of Europe ruled by Germany, or the eastern portion of Europe ruled
by Russia; and half of Europe was better than none. Charmley's knowledge of the Second World War is flawed and limited.

This brings me to his second shortcoming: the selective
character of his argumentation and of his material.* His book

---

* Major General Mackesy was an overcautious British commander in
the disastrous Norway campaign (for which Churchill was at least
partly responsible) in 1940. Churchill criticized Mackesy (in two sen-

is only partly "a political biography," as its subtitle states. Charmley spends long chapters and pages on Churchill's psyche. "Churchill's self-education . . . provided no training in learning how to think, how to weigh arguments, and how to judge your own ideas against those of others." He was marked by "egotism and naiveté." "Such egotism is common in children, but it has usually been rubbed away by the time adulthood is reached." "Truth was inconvenient for his version of history." "He was always apt to become the slave of his own ideas and to assume that to annunciate a brilliant phrase was to solve a problem." "Showman as he was, stalking through the bomb-sites with taurine glares of defiance, massive cigar stuck firmly in his mouth, he became the mythical 'Good ole Winnie.'" (No one ever called him *ole Winnie*.) Etc., etc. This is not the proper revisionism of a historian; it is a denigration by a pamphleteer.

Worrisome has been the reception of Charmley's book among defenders of the Third Reich in Germany, Austria, Hungary, and elsewhere. The heavy tome impressed some by its sheer bulk and "scholarly equipment"; it served as a quarry

---

tences) in his War Memoirs. Mackesy's son Piers, a historian, was Charmley's first tutor, "who first showed me what a historian could be." In *The End of Glory* there are five pages and ten references to Churchill's quarrel with that incompetent general, while there is but one single sentence about the Hitler-Stalin Pact in 1939 and one other sentence about the flight to England in 1941 of Rudolf Hess (who was Hitler's deputy) in this book, one of the main theses of which is the potentiality of peace with Hitler at that time. A very peculiar ratio for a historian.

which all kinds of unsavory people may mine for their special purposes. It had its critics; but not enough attention has been directed to its details, including many factual mistakes, most of them results of Charmley's special pleading. This leads me to his third shortcoming, his employment of his sources. Its evidences are latent in the many thousands of his notes — fifty-one pages in very small type. There he, often slyly, inserts attacks on historians with whom he disagrees, while praising those with whom he agrees. Churchill's official biographer, Martin Gilbert, "prints only extracts [of a document] which supports his contention." (A Pot Calling the Kettle Black!) On the American Kimball, whose commentaries of the Churchill-Roosevelt correspondence include a mass of errors, Charmley bestows the epithet of "Homer"; but then Kimball's interpretation of the Churchill-Roosevelt relationship often accords with Charmley's. A more deplorable symptom of Charmley's use of sources lies in his not infrequent dependence on David Irving. (He cites Irving often, mostly in his notes, but Irving is omitted from his index.) Like Churchill's father, who was "bank-rolled by his Jewish friends," Winston was "certainly bank-rolled by wealthy Jews" and funded by an "ardent Zionist." All of this Charmley culled from Irving. "So was Churchill the 'hired help' [Irving's words used by Charmley] for a Jewish lobby which, regarding Jewish interests as superior to those of the British Empire, was determined to embroil that Empire in a war on their behalf?" He tucks in a footnote: "Mr. Irving is cited only when his sources have been checked and seem reliable. . . . The present author admires Mr. Irving's assiduity, energy, and courage, even if he differs from him in his conclusions." The difference between John Charmley and David Irving may be a difference of degree; it may not be quite enough for a difference in kind.

Churchill had his faults. He had his sycophants, and opportunists rallied to his side when that seemed timely. His greatest virtue was his magnanimity. "Bygones are bygones," he said, again and again. He forgave many, much, and easily. He was often moved to tears, of which he was not ashamed. His daughter wrote to him in 1951: "It is hardly in the nature of things that your descendants should inherit your genius — but I earnestly hope that they may share in some way the qualities of your heart."*

---

*Quoted in Martin Gilbert, *Winston S. Churchill*, Boston, 1988, 8: 1365.

8

Two recent biographies

In the first year of the twenty-first century two significant biographies of Churchill appeared. They are different; their authors' inspirations to write them were different. But perhaps it is therefore that they are significant. Why this continued interest in Churchill? What is it that appeals to a Liberal Democrat (formerly Labour) politician; or to a professional historian whose previous books were devoted to British history in other, earlier centuries?

Roy Jenkins's *Churchill* is essentially a political biography.* Geoffrey Best's *Churchill: A Study in Greatness* is a study of character.† Jenkins had written a massive biography of Gladstone. When he started his *Churchill,* he writes at the end,

> I thought that Gladstone was, by a narrow margin, the greater man, certainly the more remarkable specimen of humanity. In the course of writing it I have changed my mind.

*Roy Jenkins, *Churchill,* London, 2001.
†Geoffrey Best, *Churchill: A Study in Greatness,* London, 2001.

I now put Churchill, with all his idiosyncrasies, his indul-
gences, his occasional childishness, but also his genius, his
tenacity and his persistent ability, right or wrong, successful
or unsuccessful, to be larger than life, as the greatest human
being ever to occupy 10 Downing Street. (912)

A Study in Greatness is the subtitle of Best's excellent book.
Still: what is "greatness"? What kind of greatness?

At the very beginning of his book Jenkins estimates the
number of those who have written on and around Churchill
as "somewhere between 50 and 100" (ix). In 2001 a research
librarian informed me that "in a broad sense — that is, not just
biographies but also works of history, fiction, juvenile literature, and works that may be about them but also about other
individuals" — books about Churchill in the United States
amounted to 283, in Canada 206, in Britain 652, in the Library
of Congress 736. In every one of these statistics (including Britain) books about Hitler outnumber those about Churchill, often two to one; so do books about Roosevelt (except for Canada
and Britain); except for the Library of Congress, Stalin runs
fourth, behind Churchill. There is an odd whiff of reality in
these computerized and otherwise meaningless statistics. Had
it not been for Hitler, in the history of Britain (not to speak of
the world) Churchill would have been a perhaps interesting
but surely secondary figure: and we may presume that Roy
Jenkins would have not chosen him for the subject of a monu-
mental biography, as he had done for Gladstone and Asquith.
Had it not been for Hitler . . . For a long time most people
were inclined to think that, of course, Churchill was brave and
resolute in 1940, but, after all, Hitler was bound to lose the

war. That he was not bound to lose it, that in 1940 and 1941 he had come very near to winning it, has become gradually apparent to more people than a few specialist military historians. Churchill knew that in the marrow of his bones—which explains much of his strategy, including his constant and fearful appreciation of the fighting abilities of the Germans.

There has been a recent tendency to describe Churchill as complicated and elusive. Complicated he may have been, but elusive? Not at all. Hitler, Roosevelt, Stalin were much more secretive than was Churchill, who spurted out many of his innermost thoughts and speculations to his staff, indeed to whomever was listening. As Jenkins puts it, "Churchill's life was singularly lacking in inhibition or concealment" (xi). That was, is, and certainly remains an asset for his biographers.

In his preface Jenkins writes: "I can at least claim to be the only octogenarian who has ventured to write about Churchill." His book is too long, but there is not much that is aged and creaky in his writing. Jenkins's ear shows none of the aural deficiencies of old age; he knows well who to listen to and then cite and when. (Churchill *circa* 1907: "I refuse to be shut up in a soup kitchen with Mrs. Sidney Webb" [108].) Jenkins has a few memorable phrases of his own (example: Churchill's decision to sink the French warships at Oran: "Nearly anyone else would have let sleeping ships lie, and hoped vaguely for the best" [624]).

To the above-cited prefatory sentence Jenkins adds: "I suppose I can also claim to have had the widest parliamentary and ministerial experience of his biographers." Yes, but there is some trouble with that. Early in his career Churchill, ac-

cording to Jenkins, "showed slight signs of parliamentary incontinence" (74). There are marks of literary incontinence in
this book. Jenkins displays too much of his knowledge of parliamentary history; too many quotes from Gladstone and Asquith; too many comparisons of electoral arithmetic; there are
long pages that deal not with Churchill but with the Conservative Party; there is too much about the Churchills' relationship
with his literary agent, Reves (and Mrs. Reves). There is also
a surprising intrusion of recent Americanisms ("networking,"
"upwardly mobile," "window of opportunity"), and an often
unnecessary sprinkling of French phrases, sometimes mis-
spelled.

They do not much matter. The book could have been cut,
but its main merit is a comprehension of Churchill's complexity — no, not elusiveness! (About his parents: "It is remarkable
that the offspring of two such old libertines should have made
one of the most famously long-lasting and faithful marriages
in history" [136].) There is a duality in every human being, but
a balanced judgment of that is perhaps the best evidence of a
biographer's talent. Jenkins understands this. Here is a prime
example of his treatment of what is perhaps *the* duality in
Churchill's character: the hedonist and the warrior. In December 1944 Churchill, weary and worn, chose to forgo the
pleasure of a quiet Christmas with his family and flew off to
a cold and dark scene in Greece. That was, to Jenkins,

> the triumph of duty over pleasure, and that, in spite of his
> self-indulgent tastes, was part of the pattern of his life.
> Whenever the two came into head-on conflict, if the issue
> was big enough, he always came down on the dutiful side.

And this, like a lot of obvious explanations, contains a large part of the truth, although not all of it. Duty always had a most powerful ally in the shape of his desire to be at the centre of events, his preference of danger over boredom, for risk over inertia. (771)

This is very good. Jenkins also knows the limitations of some of Churchill's contemporary critics. On that most dramatic of days, 18 June 1940, a day, too, of one of Churchill's greatest speeches, Jenkins quotes the acerbic Alec Cadogan: "Winston not there — writing his speech." "He might as well have complained that Lincoln did not apply himself to some minor piece of White House business on the morning of the Gettysburg Address" (621). He is also right about the Alanbrooke diaries: "Brooke's exasperation with Churchill, although combined with underlying respect, sometimes conjoined with his natural asperity to make his comments on the Prime Minister unduly harsh" (734–735).

Jenkins knew Churchill; he was involved in British political life for decades. Best, now a retired professor in Oxford, had never met Churchill — except mentally, but that made all the difference in the world. He had admired Churchill when he was very young, and then chose to write a life of his revered hero almost a half-century later. Yet his book is not a hagiography but a starry accomplishment. He read and pondered. "And all through those years I could not help becoming aware that [Churchill was] a more complicated and, in some respects, a more contradictory character than, way back in the first place, I would have thought possible" (x). Churchill once said: "I should have made nothing if I had not made mistakes."

Appropriately, this is the motto of Best's book: perhaps the best one-volume — and not unduly long — biography of Churchill.

It is very well written; it is comprehensive; and it is marked by the modesty and the sureness of its author — an attractive and unusual combination of qualities. "I have been pleased to adopt other writers' judgements when they have said things better than I could have done or have at any rate said them first. . . . Regarding the many aspects of Churchill's life which have become matters of persisting controversy, however, I have enjoyed making my own mind up" (xi). One of his emphases is that Churchill was a democratic war leader, who respected the War Cabinet and the House of Commons.

There are at least two unusual assets in Best's *Churchill*. One of them is his interest in and his extensive treatment of the private Churchill and of his family life. Here, for example, is a fine description of Churchill as he had become in the late 1920s:

> In personal terms, he was now well into his fifties and had acquired a more impressive presence than when he was younger. The body was a bit bulkier, the rather large balding head on top of it less disproportionate than it once had been; his face was fatter, readily delivering the chubby, saucy looks which encouraged the impression that he was always good-humoured and nice to everybody. In fact, he was not always nice to everybody. (142)

Best puts a valuable, and important, emphasis on the person of Clementine Churchill, and what she meant to her husband.

She was a steadying influence often through his life. It was an extraordinary marriage. There were passing problems, at times magisterially summed up by Best: "Churchill enormously enjoyed his time at the Admiralty. (How much Clementine enjoyed it is another matter)" (43). But Churchill's love for his wife endured and endured, while it "was deep and disinterested from the start . . . demonstrated to the material-minded, commonplace members of Edwardian Society by his marrying a relatively indigent young woman." (Best cites, among others, Beatrice Webb, who, *mirabile dictu,* wrote in her diary in 1908 of lunch "with Winston C. and his bride — a charming lady, well bred and pretty, and earnest withal — but not rich, by no means a good match, which is to Winston's credit") (29).

The other, perhaps unusual, quality of Best's character study derives from this erudite professor's knowledge of literature (as already evident in Best's excellent *Mid-Victorian Britain,* 1971). He understands how a novelist's — or a poet's — words and phrases may enrich a historical narrative; as Alfred Duff Cooper once wrote, "the penetrating eye of genius can discern much that remains elusive to the patient researches of a historian." Geoffrey Best's researches and reading were surely patient, but he also had the eye — and the ear — to find and respond to the penetrating words of genius. Thus his evocative narrative of Churchill's funeral, which he ends with a reminiscence that I had missed in my memories with which this book will end. "For the millions whose link with the funeral had to be television, the most unforgettable moment was probably (as it certainly was for me) the great cranes along the south side of the stretch of the river between Tower Bridge and London Bridge, dipping their masts in tribute as the launch went by 'like giants bowed in anxious thought'" (327).

"Like giants bowed in anxious thought"! Those were Churchill's words describing the somber movement of the great ships of the First Fleet through the English Channel on 28 July 1914. They must have lit a spark in Best's eye on that dark January afternoon in 1965; they must have rung in Best's ear as he was laying down his pen, ending his book. He knew an immortal passage when he read one.

9

Churchill's funeral

Churchill died on 24 January 1965 (sixty years to the day that his father had died in 1895). I was a visiting professor in the University of Toulouse, in France. I was suddenly impelled to fly to London for Churchill's funeral. My wife was not allowed to fly; but I brought my son, then eight years old, to have his memory of a great historic event. Here is my very personal, and perhaps unduly sentimental, account of our three days in London.

January Twenty-Ninth
Friday

It is a very quiet London, a humdrum day. No sense of crowds, no excitement, no feeling of something big and ceremonial. Even at the airport there are not many people; it is a winter arrival day; the kings and the prime ministers are chauffered away quickly, silently; there is little of that raincoated and gumsoled rushing around them of slovenly photographers with their hanging ogling equipment. The English are, of course, very good at this quick and efficient whisking of important people out of sight. Still it is very different from the June atmosphere of coronations, and even of royal funerals.

That gray airport bus, through the western suburbs of the great city. It is a long and humdrum approach through what were not so long ago solidly respectable rows of houses but which bear some of the outward marks of social decay. There is not much traffic in this snow and driving sleet. Past the huge dumb-impassive square aluminum buildings set up by construction companies, indistinguishable from American ones. And then, rather suddenly, near the end of the new concrete highroad, rows of brown brick buildings, a Victorian English sea of houses after the gray wintry continental cloudiness of the motorway. The lights burn yellow through the mist now, at eleven in the morning. And everywhere what, for a writer, must be one of the most evocative things of all: the inscriptions of London. The street signs and the shop fascia, the bus stops and the public lettering, most of it in that already traditional and very English modern sans-serif which Eric Gill created in 1928, I think, for the London transport system and which was, indeed, one of the few fine achievements of the English creative spirit between the wars. Of all countries that I know, England has the finest public lettering.

At first this is curious that this should be so, for an unrhetorical and unintellectual people. At second thought it is perhaps not so surprising at all. This people, with all of its Old Testament traditions, is not really a pharisaic people: with their respect for The Law there is mixed a deep strain of their love for The Word. That is why Perfidious Albion is, really, a mistaken phrase; that is why this is the Shakespearean nation; that is why they understood Churchill when he had to be understood, in that dramatic moment of their long existence.

But there are very few signs of the funeral now, less than twenty-four hours before it will begin.

The flags are at half-mast, of course. But there are not so many of them.

Noon. We walk out from the hotel, not quite sure where we shall presently head to.

It is still sleeting and gray. Hyde Park stretches out, green, wet, and empty. The traffic on the great street has dropped down to a Sunday-afternoon level; many empty cabs and only the red buses lumbering past without rumbling, much like English middle-class spinsters who had grown to maturity in the King Edward age, with a Queen Alexandra bearing, and now often their conductors are young black women and men.

We walk somewhat hesitantly eastward, into the wind. Then one notices the many different national flags, at half-mast, flying from the buildings. This row, fifty years ago the townhouses and the flats of a rich upper middle class, during the short peachy-creamy period of Peter Pan Kensington, houses many consulates now; the banners of many unknown new African countries, and Tito's red star flapping in the wind. (He, too, owes much to Churchill.)

There is something else, too. Something that towers, kindly, over the white Kensington houses with their now tattered fluorescent and bureaucratic insides. This thing stands above the intrusive, the uncomfortable thoughts of what the James Barries and the inevitable reaction to them — Bloomsbury, a tad later — had done to the spirit of England. The building which now houses the Dutch legation. It is a large red apartment building, built in the Queen Anne style, I presume, around 1910; its white curved roof gables have a Dutch impression, though this is surely coincidental. Set back from the pavement behind a low wall and a small gravely courtyard, this house stands like a large solid ship, anchored forever. Its brick walls have a tinge of vermilion; as with all colors, this impression is inseparable from the association which goes with it, that of quiet, reddish small square rooms inside, with dark comfortable furniture and brass fenders. Above the doorway, with its crest with the Royal Netherlands seal, flies the bourgeois red-white-blue horizontal flag of Holland, half-mast, in mourning.

It stands but a few hundred feet from Hyde Park Gate, from another, even more English, red-brick house where Winston Churchill died. And now, for the first time, I am gripped by the kind of emotion which is compounded by historical memory and personal association. This London house, and the Holland Legation, and Churchill — they are, all three, a monument of decency, commingled now in my mind and before my eyes. Large, tolerant, solid, and decent — this is what they stood for. Houses like this have buttressed the now-so-ramshackle edifice of a thousand years of European civilization, during its last great Protestant and Northwestern and bourgeois phase. Holland and England. Marlborough and Churchill; Holland the first England; England the second Holland; brown warm rooms and Edwardian Queen Anne; nations of families, presided over by royal families, by decent and unpretentious ones. The Dutch mourn Churchill, they understand how he tried to save a certain kind of civilization.

From the house of the Holland Legation we now drive to Westminster Hall.

The cab rolls by an endless queue. We come upon it suddenly, on Millbank, as it stretches out of the New Palace Yard and from Westminster Hall; its thousands of people stand straight and somber, huddling from the wind, scuffling slowly, close against the iron railings, way down Millbank; and then the queue is turned inward, through the small flat garden between the street and the eastern end of Westminster and the river embankment; and then it turns back again, a little sparser but long, very long. It goes all the way to the Lambeth Bridge. This will take hours. My eight-year-old son is wearing cotton socks. Still, we'll see. With a cold empty feeling in my stomach I pay off the cab on the Lambeth Bridge and there we are, in the queue.

It is a good queue because it is moving. The wind is awfully cold, blowing from the gray sheet of the Thames, but there is not that sense of hopeless democratic impatience as when one has to stand and wait and stand and wait for what seem to be endless minutes without explanation. I am surprised how far we have progressed in fifteen minutes, how long already the queue is behind us. And it is a good queue because it is an English queue, disciplined and good-natured, without jostling. After fifteen minutes I know that we'll go through with it. Behind us a group of schoolgirls, with impossibly long scarves, are joking and occasionally snickering, but somehow this does not seem out of place here: a grim, self-conscious solemnity would be. We are standing and walking and standing and walking, surrounded by a variety of people, most of them working-class, charwomen perhaps. They must know that we are not English. Paul wishes to tell them that we have flown over from Toulouse for the funeral but I dissuade him. We are not English. I came because of my conviction of respect and my sentiment of gratitude: to suggest their appreciation of us would compromise the conviction and the sentiment.

The papers wrote later that in the crowd lived the spirit of '40, that there was a great democratic upsurge of Englishmen, with men in bowler hats and elegant women standing in line with the cockneys and the stevedores. Perhaps. I don't know about that. It might have been that way, in the cold evenings and at night, in the pubs and the teashops behind Westminster where the frozen fragments of the crowd went to restore themselves with a warm cup of something. The way I see this queue is that of pale knots of different people, a long quilted afghan made out of patches of multifarious humanity: schoolgirls, working people, businessmen, and the cheap-furred, straight-backed women of the conservative middle class, a few foreigners here and there, including a few dark faces, smiling Pakistanis or Malayans. For a moment I feel a slight irritation: what do *they* have to do here? mere curiosity seekers, wanting to be present at the ceremonies of the Great Imperial Guru? But I dismiss the thought in a moment: because it is ungenerous and unreasonable: in *this* cold wind, through *this* frozen garden, for such hours, it is wrong, absolutely wrong, to question motives.

The working people. We have now made the first turn in the queue and people are talking. The charwomen. (But are they charwomen?) In their greenish old tweed coats, the brown wool scarves, the little glasses resting on the bumps of their pale faces, their bad teeth, their thin mouths. "I was here in 'Forty." "There was St. Paul's with all the City blazing around it, you know." But these are standard memories which have been repeated over and over again, presumably in the papers all through this week. How much of the memories are real? How much a mixture of associations? It doesn't matter. What matters is that they came, in this cold, which is no ceremony and no coronation, a hundred thousand of the working people of England, with their good nature and their knobby faces, out of a still-living feeling rather than of memory — to the bier of a man who led them not to a great victory but who saved them from the worst of possible defeats, from the collapse of English self-respect.

Now their houses are warm and their television is going and they live better than ever before . . . Better: well, in a way. And they sense, too, the transitory malleability of this comfort, the old working people of old England, the tired members of the island race even in this airplane age: still members, not fragments: selfish but self-respecting: unimaginative but fair. *Fair.* One day when the last portions of the green fairness of England will be gone or meticulously fenced in by planners and antiquarians, that old green fairness will still exist, I think: it is the green copper bottom of the hearts of the working people of England.

But the middle class is here, too. And my heart goes out for them.

I mean the middle class, and not the more elegant members of the upper middle class. I mean men in their thin towncoats, women with their bony cheeks and blue eyes who have already lived longer than they shall live, erect and tired; I do not mean the children of Saki, the men and women of the once world of Evelyn Waugh and of the boring world of Anthony Powell. I need not describe them. I mean the people who were once the backbone of England.

It is a strange thing: but they, the upholders of the Conservative Party and of the once Imperial Spirit and of the Country Right Or Wrong, were not those to whom Churchill meant the most. Like all of the really grands seigneurs, Churchill was closer to the aristocracy and also to the lower classes of the people. To the lower classes not because he had much of the vulgar demagogue in him (earthy he could be but rarely vulgar) but because the lower classes sometimes instinctively understood him even on his terms, on his own level. (In a news film I once saw a flick of a Churchill gesture that I cannot forget. He is coming through the ruins of an East London street after one of the bombardments. There are people, including a woman, with blowing hair, like the spirit of a proletarian Boadicea, running up to him from the ruins, gathering around him as he marches through the rubble in his tall hat and coat and cane, smoking with his incomparable chewing smile. As one of them runs up, he pats her on the back with his left arm, with a There, there! There, there! gesture. It is an amiable, patronizing, and nonchalant everyday gesture. For a moment one senses that feeling of utter trust and confidence which only certain grandfathers can give.)

It was at that time – October 1940? – that the gray ice on the faces of the middle class melted enough to reveal a racial facet of their true selves. He infused some kind of a sense into their long decline, from Kensington to Kensington. They were not the lot of hard-faced men who had made out well from the first war: but they were, let's face it, the people of Baldwin and of Chamberlain, stiff and unimaginative, with a tight kind of patriotism that was no longer enough. It was not merely a clique of narrow Germanophile politicians who distrusted Churchill in the thirties, it was the once large middle class of England who instinctively distrusted him: they were the people who had a natural trust in the Chamberlains: Churchill's pugnacity, his rhetoric, his brilliance, his Francophilia, and his Americanisms – these were things they shunned, uneasily, stiffly, shyly. Then, in 1940, all of this flashed away. Even then they did not quite understand him: but in this country of common sense this was irrelevant then, and it is irrelevant still. For after the war, it was this thinning and threadbare and sorely tried middle class that continued to believe in some of the older patriotic virtues no matter how out of date these seemed to have become. Slowly, instinctively, through their bones – their bones warmed by this feeling through the chilly austerity years of British decline – their minds received Churchill, with his prose and through the memories of the war.

Oh, this shy race of men and women, how very different they are from other middle classes of other nations, from the bourgeois of the Continent! They are shy because they are kind. Kindness is not yet generosity, just as fairness isn't all honesty. But it is still from among their children that there may come forward one day an angry and generous Englishman, at another great dark hour of civilization, an avenging angel remembering Churchill.

Now, in his death, the pomp means less to them than to the others; it is not the might and the parade, the flags and the bands that impress them, but they, perhaps for the first time, have an inner comprehension of the magnanimity of this man now dead. Now, in his death, he belongs to them perhaps even more than to anyone else in England.

Nineteen-forty is close now: the volunteer vans. We have turned away from the Thames; we are in the line moving slowly toward Millbank. There are three old blue vans of a volunteer service parked on the grass, and old small women address us with paper cups, offering blackish tea and Bovril. Two of the vans bear these inscriptions in small white paint: "London 1940–44. Coventry 1940. Bristol 1941." Nineteen-forty is close now; and the soft little rumble of the long queue seems to have dropped.

It is perhaps an appropriate thing that the American delegation to this Churchill funeral, because of some kind of Washington complexity and confusion, is unimpressive and second-rate. It is appropriate because 1940 has no great meaning for Americans. Nineteen-forty is a high year, a historic date, a sharp and poignant association for Britain and for Europe, not for America. There was, of course, Churchill's romantic Americanism, the very, very necessary help that Roosevelt chose to give him at that time, the sympathy, the interest, the willingness that millions of Americans had for Britain's struggle late that summer. But 1940 was still the peak of the European War, before America, Russia, Japan entered the scene; it was the gripping great crisis of the civilization of Europe rather than that of the "West" (a word hurriedly resuscitated and put into currency only after 1945) or, at that, of the United Nations. The lines were clear in 1940. Hitler, Mussolini, Stalin, the Japanese, the opportunists as well as the Jew haters, the Anglophobes of the lower middle classes, oily Spanish functionaries as well as the dark peasant masses of Russia—they, all, had their mean little enjoyments in witnessing the humiliations of Britannia. The other side was incarnated by Churchill, simply and clearly. It was good to know that summer—and not only for the British—that the struggle was ineluctable; that even in this century where everything is blurred by the viscous wash of public relations, there were still two camps as close to Good Versus Evil as ever in the terrestrial struggles of nations.

All of this touched the United States but indirectly. This is even true of the great English speeches of Churchill that year. Despite the evocative power of the same—or, rather, of almost the same—language, his great June and July resolution meant something much more to certain Europeans than to Americans then. I say "certain Europeans" because at that time many of them were only small minorities, those who knew they lived in the dark, who had lived to see Hitler triumphant, who had experienced the quick sinking of a new kind of iron night on their once civilized evenings. They were the ones who needed the most that spirit of defiance and of inspiration and of British self-confidence which Churchill alone gave.

Westminster Hall. First there is the sense of relief from the cold, the sleet and wind dropping behind one in an instant; it is mingled with that other sense of relief that the long cold progress is over. Here, for the first time, the gestures of the policemen are quicker. The crowd surges forward for a moment, many abreast, on the steps — and there we are, formed into two lines, in a hall. We are already moving to the left. It is very simple. In that enormous hall, under its English Gothic beams, a very tall catafalque, like a great memorial stone cut in dull black, and his coffin under a large generous British flag. The rest is what one would expect: the four Royal Marines standing like statues, and the tall candles burning.

So there we go, rather quickly now; and as we come closer I sense that the catafalque is perhaps purposely higher than usual, the flag larger than usual, which is why it is so fitting. There lies an old corpulent man whose flesh had begun to dissolve some time ago. He loved life very much; and he made life possible for many of us because he had a very old, and very strong, belief in the possibilities of human decency and of human greatness. History is not a record of life but life itself: because we are neither human animals nor perpetual slaves. In the long and slow and sad music of humanity he once sounded an English and noble note which some of us were blessed to receive and to remember.

Now up the stairs and before us we see the open door where the crowds file through and immediately dissolve, taken up by the stream of everyday London. But:

instinctively, at the top of the stairs, everyone of us turns around, for a moment. I wrote "us" because, for the first and only time, I felt that I can write this honestly: not an Englishman, my grief was different from theirs, but at this moment — this very individual moment, since there is, curiously, not a speck of crowd psychic reaction in this turning around — we are all one. Again the tall catafalque and the candles blowing and the four ceremonial guards and the flag covering the coffin, all palely shining through the thin light which comes in through the large window, with its small and reconstituted unimpressive stained-glass panels. It is not perhaps the scene which is unforgettable: it is the occasion. Farewell Churchill. Farewell British Empire. Farewell, spiritual father. Of many. Including myself.

January Thirtieth
Saturday

The thirtieth of January. Dawn thoughts. On this day Franklin Roosevelt was born in 1882, and Adolf Hitler came to power in Germany thirty-two years ago.

Roosevelt and Hitler died within the same month, in April 1945. Churchill survived them by twenty years. His relationship with Roosevelt was a complex one: a mixture of genuine affection (on Churchill's part, that was), a strong recognition of obligations, a sense of loyalty together with what was a very

Churchillian unwillingness to fight for certain things. It is difficult to say what were the deeper sources of his unusual deference to Roosevelt during the last two years of the war: his absolute conviction of the necessity of American benevolence for Britain, together with a certain weariness, played a role in that. Roosevelt, in turn, was the smaller person of the two — not because of his breezy American seignorialism shining at times on his face (that Churchill liked) but because of a certain uneasiness toward Churchill (and toward Britain, Europe, history) — a compound of sentiments of inferiority and of superiority, the by-products of a Rooseveltian intellectual attitude which professed to see the twentieth century as The Century of America and of the Common Man: in these terms Churchill was a brave roast beef Tory, an almost Dickensian figure. This was the same kind of American myopia which made Oliver Wendell Holmes consider Harold Laski to have been the greatest brain in England. Still, in 1940 at least, Roosevelt's heart was in the right place. Hence Churchill's enduring gratitude too.

Much has been written about Hitler's love-hate relationship with England. In reality, this theme is overdone. This evil genius, capable of great instinctive flashes of comprehension when dealing with some of the motive forces of various national characteristics, never understood the English, and least of all did he understand Churchill. He did not understand that behind This Far And No Further there was something more than a stubborn dumb pragmatism; he could not understand the romantic springs of English sentiment; he mistook Churchill's bravery for mere panache; Churchill's peculiar compound of resolution and nonchalance was one of the few things which remained far beyond the reach of Hitler's wild and powerful mind.

Churchill and Hitler were, at any rate, the two protagonists of the dramatic phase of the last war, even though Roosevelt and Stalin played the decisive roles in its epic phase, in the end.

A young man was supposed to have said yesterday: "Let's hope that Hitler can see this now."

But the crowds are not big. Four, five deep at the most. And how silent they are. We had risen early, in a black dawn; dressed and walked down to the Gloucester Road. The streets had a quiet Sunday feeling. A few polite posters telling motorists that some of the Thames bridges will be closed for the funeral. But the Underground is running — the Underground, with its sultana-cake plush seats, with its peculiar coal-and-cocoa smell. At Westminster Station we rose to the surface, into the jaws of the large long crowd — and great, great quiet, well an hour before the great procession was to move out of the New Palace Yard.

I read later, and heard it discussed on the plane back to Paris by a famous American reporter, that what had impressed him was the pride of the crowd, that this was a day of great inner pride, that the people of England had pulled themselves up this week and showed a proud face to the world in their mourning. This is not what I saw. Perhaps certain foreigners, television reporters, Americans felt this, because of some of their preconceived ideas: but foreigners, and especially

Americans (this is strange) are prone to mistake the English aloofness for some kind of haughtiness instead of seeing what it is: the essential shyness of this people. I saw less pride than a kind of disciplined resignation, and a respectful sadness: a sadness full of the remembrance of the past for those who had memories of 1940; and, for the young, full of a strange, vague, almost medieval respect for a distant and legendary figure, someone removed even from their parents' generation, some-one with real authority, someone they could respect . . . That was strange: the papers remarked it, too: the large number of young people in the crowds, long-haired, sad-faced young bar-barians, in search for something, with their strange, watery eyes.

For the others self-respect rather than pride, and a self-respect tinted with the sense of passing time. There was in this a thin thread of resigned realization that for *this* England, in her present situation, the Churchillian generation was too old: that he was the right man at the right time but not for the gray, the difficult, the technical present. I do not think that there are very many Englishmen, including Conservatives, who re-gard the election of July 1945 which turned Churchill out of power as some kind of a national disaster. They have an in-stinctive feeling that he was right for the war rather than for the postwar time. (And this is true in a way: with all of his great gifts, with his great understanding of world history, with his great insights into movements, connections, correspondences, tendencies, Churchill was not a good diplomatist — especially not when it came to dealing with Americans . . .)

A Churchillian generation: there was, really, no such thing.

Eden, Beaverbrook, Macmillan, Duff Cooper . . . Duff Cooper
was close to Churchill in spirit: but he never had more than
a minor position. The shock that grips all of England at this
moment is the sight of Macmillan, Eden, Attlee, among the
honorary pallbearers. How infinitely old they look! Attlee is
bent over twice. He has to sit down in the cold wind, in a big
black overcoat, protected carefully by a tall Guards officer.
Then, for a moment, Eden — infinitely old, infinitely weary,
too — bends over Attlee with a kind of great solicitude. It shows
how far away we are now from the Churchillian Days, from
the time of the Low cartoon of May 1940, "We're all behind
you, Winston!" — Attlee, Bevin, Morrison, Greenwood, all of
them rolling up their sleeves and marching in a broad file behind Churchill. Low drew them (how well I remember that
cartoon) in a somewhat unimaginative outfit, like English shop
stewards in their Sunday best they looked. But they were, at
that moment, the good, the reliable, the last best hope, the
shop stewards of European civilization.

The RAF pilots escorting the coffin. "Never in the field of human conflict was so much owed by so many to so few." That
was, to some extent, a Churchillian exaggeration. (His 1940
rhetoric was not always exaggerated, the "We shall fight in the
streets" passage, for example: there are witnesses to whom he
had said in May that if the Germans were to land and push
into London he would go with a rifle to the sentry box at the
end of Downing Street and keep firing at them 'til the end.)
Would the Battle of Britain have been won without American
support? I do not mean the material support, which was not

decisive at that time; I mean the knowledge, by Churchill and by the people of England and by the world, that America was moving away from neutrality, toward their side. And the legendary figures announced in 1940 *were* exaggerated. "You can always take one of them with you": the RAF pilots *did* take more than one of them but not five or six. The score was a little less than two to one. Still, it was an appropriate thing to have the officers of the 1940 fighter squadrons form the first escort. They are grandfathers now, most of them; slightly corpulent training officers in pacific command posts; it is not difficult to imagine their suburban homes, their habits, their families. They have nothing of Valhalla heroes' marks on their faces. They, in 1940, they only did their duty, they would say. Now, too.

The Polish officer. He is in the crowd, with his Slavic, creased face, in an angular black suit, wearing the ribbons of his medals. So this man came to pay his respects, too. For a long time the exiled Poles were bitter about Churchill. They had reason to be. From the very beginning he had found it necessary to compromise with Stalin. He wanted to let the Russians have the eastern portion of Poland up to the Curzon (or, rather, Lloyd George) Line, in exchange for a Russian agreement for a Russophile but free Polish government. In this he failed: in the end Stalin got both the frontier and the government he wanted, a big Soviet Ukraine and a subservient Communist regime in Warsaw. At Yalta, too, Churchill fought for the cause of Poland and lost (he won for France instead). Having lost, he put up a good front and went far in defending Yalta in the House of Commons. How bitter it must have been for the brave Polish exiles, with their large wounded army, these months in the ruined 1945 landscape of London! They had fought and bled in three continents, for six years, and they were abandoned in the end: large Russian armies installed forever in the terrible landscape of their ravaged country, and with the acquiescence of Churchill. (The Yugoslav exiles fared worse: Churchill had put his chips on the bandit Tito well before the end of the war.)

A German Christian-Democrat newspaper in Bonn, paying homage to Churchill, wrote among other things that he was nevertheless responsible for the division of Europe, having let Stalin come far into the heart of the Continent. And yet that is all wrong. Churchill tried to save what he could. At least his basic idea was right, as it was indeed in 1915, in the Dardanelles business, even though he could not carry it out — in 1915 because of the British government, in 1943–1945 because of the distrust of the American government. Churchill knew that a price had to be paid in Eastern Europe for the Russian contribution to Germany's defeat; also, he knew the Russians better than did Roosevelt, knowing that this price ought to be fixed in advance, for with the Russians no postponing of unpleasant things and no vague declarations of universal goodwill would do. He was more concerned with the tragic destinies of Poland than Roosevelt, who was, at worst, concerned with his Polish-American voters, and Hull, who pleaded moral indignation in refusing to enter into Territorial Deals. And when in October 1944 Churchill, exasperated with American procrastination, sat down with Stalin and divided

with him on a sheet of paper the rest of Eastern Europe, only
a simple-witted person or some kind of a special pleader may
see in that the evidence of Traditional and Perfidious Machia-
vellian Diplomacy: for at that time, as indeed on other occasions, what Churchill did was to try to save what was possible.
And he did. He made sure that the Russians won't interfere
in Greece, which he then saved from a Communist takeover.
His support of Tito, too, paid off in a way: it contributed to
Tito's sense of his independence: surely this made the latter
less dependent on Stalin: it helped to make his future break
from Moscow possible. Even Poland remained a nation, after
all, far from being independent but, still, a nation and a state
at a time when Stalin could have done anything he wanted in
that part of Europe: he did not incorporate Poland into Russia,
after all.

In that way, too, Churchill was a great European. But how
bitter and lonely must have been those exile years to men and
women such as this angular, wooden Pole, alone for more than
two decades now in this gray and unemotional London! And
yet he is here, on this icy street, silent and stolid. What must
be the thoughts and the memories that burn slowly in that
creased, war-worn skull! Churchill and he *were* fighting com-
rades in a great European War, after all. And when I read in
the paper, next day, that Poland (Communist Poland, that is)
was the only Eastern European nation that was represented
by a cabinet minister, and that he sat in St. Paul's among the
official guests, and so did the old spare leaders of the Polish
national army, Anders and Bór-Komorowski, I thought that
this was only fitting and just, and that in issuing the invitations

to the latter the British had, instinctively, done the right (and not merely the proper) thing again.

The monarchs of Northwestern Europe. Olav of Norway (rubicund); Frederick of Denmark (genial); Baudouin of Belgium (still like a student); Jean of Luxembourg (looking surprisingly like Otto of Hapsburg); Queen Juliana (surprisingly heavy). It is right that they should be here. Churchill saved their countries twenty-five years ago.

And, so, this is a sad family occasion. They have an instinctive tie of memory with Elizabeth, who, like some of them, was very young at that time. They know what they owe to this great commoner now dead. That there is this great array of royalty paying their respects at the bier of a statesman is not the important thing. The important thing, again, is the memory of 1940: those dazzling, feverish evenings of the brilliant and deadly May and June of that year. Four times in six weeks King George and his queen had driven in the evening to Victoria Station, to greet the fleeing monarchs and presidents of Europe with dignity, sympathy, and solicitude. The German air attacks had not yet begun, and the sky was enormously blue in London, unlike those black clouds that had risen from the fires of Bergen, Rotterdam, Antwerp. In the white rooms of London hotels these royal persons of Europe were surrounded by gentleness and courtesy, by the fading flowers of a civilization. They had come to be thus received in its then last island house.

They are respectable men and women, these constitutional monarchs of the small democratic nations of Northwestern

Europe. For a moment, as they stand, some of them uneasily, on the steps of St. Paul's, they are a family unto themselves. They represent those lands of the world where there are still many living movements to an older kind of humaneness. On the surface map of the world they represent the central cluster of decency, these bourgeois monarchs of Northwestern Europe. Churchill knew that: for he was a monarchist not merely out of sentiment but because of his deep historical reason. In a fatherless world they are sources of a certain strength and of a certain inspiration. May they live and reign for long! May their presidency over the Sunday afternoons of Western Europe be prolonged!

Above them towers now de Gaulle. "The Constable of France": thus Churchill saw him in June 1940. The constable of a new Europe, then? There was something to this. His presence is regal: natural, without the slightest pomp. There he stands in his ill-fitting French army greatcoat, blinking occasionally, putting on his glasses, leaning down to Prince Jean of Luxembourg, saying something with a bearing that reflects a familiarity and solicitude. Many, many people in this great royal assembly look at him often. Later the London papers describe him in terms of unstinted admiration and respect. Very little of that uneasy suppressed dislike with which some Americans regard de Gaulle. But, of course, their quarrels and the phrase of the heavy burden of the Cross of Lorraine notwithstanding, Churchill understood and respected de Gaulle; so far as their conceptions of history (and of human nature, too) went, Churchill and de Gaulle, two national leaders of the

Right, had more in common than Churchill and Roosevelt. This is what most intellectuals failed to understand: that in 1940 the truest opponents of Hitlerism were men of the Right, not of the Left: Churchill and de Gaulle, each representing a certain superb kind of patriotism, not internationalism.

A ragged group of Frenchmen. They, as well as groups from Denmark and from elsewhere, flew over here representing their Resistance. Their silken tricolors wave smartly as the coffin moves by. These colors, together with the few red-and-white-crossed Danish flags, enlighten for a moment the somber tints of the procession, beneath the cold blackened imperial buildings of Whitehall. They are a ragged group of men and women, marching disordered as in any French civic parade, many of them paunchy, with their rimless glasses: small *fonctionnaires* and *propriétaires* (one old Frenchman with an angelic white beard shuffles on, pink-faced, waving an enormous flag).

The French owe much to Churchill. Unfortunately, not many of them recognize this. (De Gaulle does: despite the struggles and the quarrels and the high-hatted arguments in his *Memoirs,* he did write down a crucial sentence that without Churchill he and Free France would have been nothing, nothing. "Shipwrecked from desolation," he wrote, "on the shores of England, what could I have done without his help?") It is a curious thing that while elsewhere on the Continent the national traitors and the Fascist politicians were the Germanophiles, in France the party of surrender, the nationalist party, consisted of Anglophobes. Anglophobia, not Germanophilia,

was the key to the behavior and to the attitudes of Pétain, La-
val, Darlan. They had had reasons for distrusting Chamberlain: unfortunately, they distrusted Churchill even more. That
tremendous, ill-considered, but genuine Churchillian offer for
an Anglo-French Union, uttered on the sixteenth of June in
1940, was one of the strangest declarations in modern history
and in the history of Great Britain. Throughout his life
Churchill was a Francophile. This shines through not only in
his great generous gestures of 1940 (that inimitable broadcast
to the French in October: *Dieu protège la France!*) but in the
way he fought for France and for de Gaulle five years later, at
Yalta, and six years before 1940 as he spoke in the House of
Commons: "Thank God for the French Army!" he said. (He
also noted the utter annoyance and disbelief on the faces of
the members.) This was more than a political choice for
Churchill. He belonged to a generation of aristocratic and patrician Englishmen who, coming to maturity in the Edwardian
Age, were, among all British generations, the most conversant
with the political history of the Continent and the most deeply
attuned to the delights and civilities of French culture.
Churchill was never prone to take a philistine view of Europe,
not even when the Continent was ruined, when the governments of the ancient states of Western Europe had been
reduced to the role of tattered suppliants, when it seemed
that America and Britain and Russia would rule the world. His
distaste for the Birmingham municipal radicalism of the
Chamberlains was part and parcel of his distaste for the Ger-
manic inclinations and sympathies of that kind of British middle class. (His artistic inclinations reflected these tendencies,

too: his lacking interest in music, his painting in the manner of the French Impressionists.) Unlike those of some of his Edwardian contemporaries, Churchill's Francophilia was more than an acquired taste for certain pleasant and civilized delights. He enormously admired Joan of Arc and Napoleon, two of the greatest opponents of England. He understood something of what D. H. Lawrence once noted, that the Rhine was a peculiar frontier of the European spirit. He believed in the alliance, in the necessary alliance, of St. George and St. Denis; and he represented that short-lived Anglo-French conflation of spirit which, with its elegance and nonchalance, marked some of the highest levels of European civilization early in this century.

The Churchill family. Despite his aristocratic inclinations (among them his thoroughbred characteristic of impatience: the most aristocratic and least helpful of his characteristics) Churchill had a deep understanding of the patient virtues of patrician family life, of that fragment of bourgeois civilization. One must know something of the English aristocracy to recognize how unusual that was. Thus the beauty and the dignity with which his family walks behind his coffin is a living apotheosis of his personal ideals. Not a trace of that self-conscious pride which would make them a center of attention. Suicide, divorce, degradation, they have all fallen away. There are no signs of the ravages of life, only the tragic quiet of discipline on Sarah Churchill's pale jeweled face. (She is fifty years old now!) Her father would have been solicitous of her on this day.

On this day of Sabbath the British people mourn a great David-like figure who is buried with the pomp and reward of a great Old Testament Patriarch. It being Sabbath, the president of Israel couldn't ride in a car; he had to walk to St. Paul's.

That, too, is fitting for the occasion. The heads of the state of Israel walking, small and solemn, to Churchill's funeral. Enormous are the debts that the people of Israel owed, and still owe, to Churchill. I am not thinking of his support for the Jewish State, which goes back a long time. It is, all, a one-way debt. Unlike Roosevelt, he owed little to Jewish political support. Churchill had few vested interests in supporting Israel; he was a new King Cyrus without an Esther. He saw the evil incarnated in Hitler instantly, immediately. Then he rose like a hero, highest in those months in 1940 when the future of human decency was at stake, and when Jewry and Christianity were on the same side, which was the side incarnated by him, which was his side. It is therefore that no Jewish intellectual should ever call Churchill "a splendid anachronism"; it is therefore that every conscientious Catholic should pay respects to this Englishman who, in a supreme moment, saw Evil even clearer than had the Pope.

The procession has reached the Thames.

We are told that this is the end of the state funeral, and that from now on the private progress of mourning belongs to the Churchill family. In reality there is no frontier between the two portions of the procession. But the progress is thinning out. The crowds are lighter; on the bridges, closed to traffic, they are not more than three deep, and some of them will scurry across the width of the bridge to follow the watery wake of the launches.

And it is because of the royal procession melting away in the City that, somehow, the funeral becomes sadder and more poignant. There is the wail of the bagpipes, keening across the cold river: but their impression is only aleatory now. There is something very sad in the aspect of this river, and in the small neat launch that will carry Churchill's coffin upstream. It is said that he himself, in instructions he had left for his funeral, wanted his coffin to be carried up the Thames, as was Nelson's. But how different is the Thames now from Nelson's, or even Wellington's time! Two hundred years ago Canaletto himself painted it and wondered at it, when it was a great green river, ample and rich like the empire, with gardens and rich terraces on its borders. Now it is a gray and narrowing flow, with but faint memories of the ocean sea whose scummy tides race inland on dark evenings; the once rich shipping of the Port of London is sparse and far downstream. No longer could a warship, even a destroyer, come upstream for Churchill. The *Havengore* is a launch used for hydrographic tasks by the Port of London Authority.

Swiftly she sails up the cold narrowing river, bordered by warehouses, barges, and cranes. And as she is small, the coffin, covered and now protected by that large and lovely flag, is visible to all.

The train. In a black automobile, simply, the coffin is now driven to the train. The crowds are sparse now: but, still, that enormous silence, all over London.

Up to now everything connected with the arrangement of the funeral was stately and appropriate; now it has become appropriate in a familiar sense. The midday silence of the great iron railway hall, for example. Waterloo Station. That peculiarly English, steady stutterless hissing of the steam locomotive. Far on the other side of the station other trains are standing and people moving, the regular Saturday traffic of the British Railways. The train is appropriate: it brings to life the Edwardian memories, the comfortable English patrician tastes of Churchill's age: those butter-and-chocolate British Pullman cars, including the van in which the Irish Guards will place the coffin, painted cream and maroon, including the momentary sight of the tables laid in white napery with their little yellow fringed lamps in a dining car for the family, including the portly engine. In the procession there is now the sense of the few small hitches of a family occasion: the Pullman waiter, standing respectfully but somewhat uneasily in his white spencer jacket, the nervousness of the stationmaster who looks at his watch too often, because, for the first time, this perfectly managed timetable is a minute or two late.

Then — and how appropriate this is! — the locomotive blows twice. The sound of the whistle is melancholy and raucous at the same time. The steady hissing of the steam valves remains the same; there is no dramatic huffing and puffing as the train gathers speed and glides out of the iron station into the pale sunlight of the western Saturday afternoon.

In a minute its rumble dies away; the end of the last coach vanishes; now, for the first time, we are face to face with the emptiness of the afternoon.

That afternoon and evening I walked in the streets and across the squares of this great city.

Everything resumed now its course, the theatres and the cinemas and the shops were open, the football matches were played and there was racing in the wet parks, the crowds filled the streets but the sense of silence remained. I felt nothing of that inner, quiet glow of relief that so often follows funerals and other ceremonial occasions. I am sure that there were few gatherings in great houses this day; that, instead, at the same time, the inner silence was something oppressive.

There was now, in London, some of that yellow fog that, in the cold, reminds one of what one knows of the nineteenth century; of imperial London with its large Roman paving blocks, and the black processions of thousands of cabs, and the great throngs of people in the cold shadows of the stony classical buildings built by an imperial race. This dark-bright evening of London was closer to, say, 1875 than to 1935. Now the city was full, fuller than a century ago, and yet there was a sense of emptiness or, rather, an emptiness of sense: something had gone out of the spirit of these imperial buildings: Trafalgar Square was brilliantly lit, but it was not Nelson's Column and the lions which were strange: it was Admiralty Arch, that well-proportioned Edwardian building with its proud Latin inscription chiseled large and deep over the seething roadways; it seemed ancient and emptied out now.

It was because of Churchill that Macaulay's awful prediction still had not come true, that tourists from New Zealand standing on London Bridge may contemplate a large living metropolis and not merely a few broken buildings. London had risen from her partial ruins, and her imperial monuments, lit by floodlights and by the eerie sideglows of her cinemas, still stand. But it was a purposeless crowd who swirled among them on this silent evening.

Meanwhile I had a sandwich in a place called a Wimpy. The waitress in a wimpy maroon uniform was very English, with her bunlike face and her shyness and adolescent incompetence. I thought of the fat-faced advertising managers and the horde of public relations men who decide on names such as Wimpy, who spread the cheeseburger all over Britain, and the end result of their American publicity bang being a weak British wimpy.

There came in a man, a fortyish man with glasses and a mouse-colored moustache, and a turned-down mouth between a woolen scarf and his gray tired face. He may have been a teacher in a poor school in the Midlands. He looked at the plastic menu for a while. Then he said to the waitress: "A Wimpy, please." As he said that, there passed a shadow of embarrassment, a flicker of resigned disturbance across his face. I thought that I could detect something of the same on the otherwise nearly vacuous, pale face of the little waitress, too. *That* embarrassment they shared in common. Surrounded by Wimpies and the cheap metallic filth of plastic dishes and the sex magazines, in the midst of this vast process of thin liquefaction that flicker of embarrassment was a faint sign of the atavistic resistance of the race: a faint sign but a sign nonetheless: a weak glow but still a glow of the once fire, of some kind of an ember below the ashes.

January Thirty-First
Sunday

The Sunday papers. In the quiet of the morning, the Sunday papers. (All of the weariness in the civilization of the great English-speaking cities in the twentieth century lies latent in these two words and in their associations: Sunday papers.)

The long accounts of yesterday's funeral and the excellent photographs are there, but, somewhat surprisingly, the articles are not very good. There are slips even in the evocative details — one of the young leader writers saying, for example, that as the launch moved off Tower Bridge Pier, "a band crashed out with the tune that was a last Churchillian brag: 'Rule Britannia'": how wrong it is, the crash instead of the muffled keening across the long dampness, and the Last Churchillian Brag, as if it had not been something infinitely different and melancholy. There are also such things as the article by the Fellow and Director of English Studies (in reality a New York intellectual eager beaver) at Churchill College (in reality a Lord Snow institution), ending with a real Madison Avenue phrase: "Given the tools, Churchill College can do its part of the exciting job."

All through the week the writers of articles did capture many of the fragments and some of the atmosphere of the occasion: but now the reminiscences have a curious kind of nervous tiredness about them. The more intelligent among the commentators, thus, write that this funeral was indeed a proud and ceremonial occasion but the last occasion for something that is irrevocably past, the last time when London was the capital of the world: for after this last solemn homage to the glories of a British imperial past the worn weekdays of a compressed modest England begin anew. This may be true: but it does not quite explain that slight awkwardness of the eulogies by some of the more perceptive younger writers. I think I know the sources of that awkwardness of sentiment: it is the knowledge, especially of those who had grown up in the postwar years, that the Churchill victory of the Second World War was, after all, not much of a victory indeed.

That, too, may be true. But this intellectual recognition, lurking uneasily beneath the immediate impressions of the occasion, does not really conflict, for once, with the sentiments of the people: the sense of gratitude by this unemotional people of England which is now untainted either by nostalgia or by self-pity: because it has little to do with the glory of victory. It is the sense that *Churchill had saved them from defeat* rather than the knowledge that he had led Britain to victory. This is, I think, what accounts for the absence of any amount of nostalgic jingoism among the people – who, even more than the journalists and the statesmen and, of course, than the intellectuals, may feel in their bones how close England was to disaster in 1940.

Now this seems to be rather obvious: but few people, I think, comprehended its historical portents.

To most people, in England as well as abroad, the thirties are, in retrospect, something like a rather incredible episode, an era of philistine stupidity. The older generation who lived through it are not prone to analyze it in any detail, partly because of the fortunate British mental habit of letting bygones be bygones, partly because of the less fortunate British unwillingness to face certain unpleasant truths. To the younger generation it is yet another example of the myopia of the then-governing classes. The consequence of these beliefs is, then, that Churchill came forth, at a time of great distress, to attune the spirit of England to its standard condition.

But was this really so? As one contemplates the devolution of Britain during the past half-century, one gets the impression that it was the lassitude which was the standard condition, in the twenties and the thirties and the fifties and the sixties. The Bonar Laws as well as the Lansburys, the donkey generals of 1917 and the asses of the 1935 Peace Ballot, the spirit of Harold Laski as well as the Great Ideas of Lord Snow: what did they, what do they, have in common with Churchill? In one of the few fortunate phrases in the postmortems Dame Rebecca West wrote that she remembers Churchill in the twenties shining with vitality as if it had been sluiced over him with a pail. This at a time when the spirit of England had begun to smell like weak cocoa.

This does not mean that Churchill was completely isolated, absolutely alone: he was out of spirit with the *Times*, he was out of spirit with "the times" (whatever that is), but there was something else: he knew that he could bring an entire people with him, in 1940. This was one of the great differences between Churchill and de Gaulle at that time. But even this does not mean that 1940 represented England in its standard conditions. And the people know this better than the intellectuals. Hence their deep emotional regret. They know how there loomed in 1940 the possibility of something that is still unspeakable and perhaps unthinkable: that England, despite her island situation, despite the riches of her then-Empire, despite the aid from the United States, could have indeed collapsed before the strong and purposeful Germany, because England already then was at the tail end of a long period of lassitude and of abdication, because in the spirit of England, then as now, the vitality of aspirations shimmered very low.

To the current generation it seems unthinkable that Hitler could have ever won the war at all. To the intellectuals Hitlerism represents a strange, and perhaps fascinating, barbaric and reactionary episode of a temporary madness going against the broad stream of the twentieth century, against the long and broad history of mechanical progress. England, together with the United States and the Soviet Union and the Progressive Forces of the world, was bound to defeat Fascism: foolish and stupid statesmen and vested interests had led her close to great painful disasters, whereupon Churchill, who only did in great style what had to be done anyhow, restored the balance of reason and of democratic virtue with Shakespearean words and gestures; that was his role; that was all. But that wasn't it at all. People still do not know how close Hitler and his cohorts came to winning the war in 1940. Certain men and women who are attuned better to listening to the movements and the sentiments of large masses of people in Europe know this better than do the intellectuals, including certain professional historians; and the common people of England who had lived through the war sense it better, too.

They could have been conquered. Their island history would have come to an end. Their self-respect would have gone for good. Churchill saved them from this fate: and he had appealed to them as he did so. It is a mark of the decency and of the common sense of the people of England that they were not, and are not now, puffed up with pride in remembering those days, and that the stillness reigning over Churchill's funeral reflects their now profound sentiment of still gratitude to him for having done so.

Several of the men now writing about Churchill's life say that he was at his best, at his most courageous, when he was alone in the thirties, the lonely political Cassandra, the warning trumpet, the voice in the wilderness. This is an arguable proposition. Churchill, though of a small minority, was not entirely alone in the thirties; he had certain newspaper columns at his disposal; and there is, at any rate, a difference between speaking out when one has no official position at all and between leading a half-armed nation, urged by instinct, on a proud course of defiance in face of the strong possibility of disaster. And: is it really true that Hitler could have been stopped easily in 'Thirty-Eight or in 'Thirty-Six, at the time of Munich or at the time of the Rhineland? I am not so sure about that. Of course Churchill was right. But who would have followed him in 'Thirty-Six? Not Baldwin. Not Chamberlain. Not the Liberals. Not the Laborites. Not the Trade Unions. Not the Fabianists. Not the Socialists. Not the Pacifists. Not the Popular Front. Not the Commonwealth. Not the Americans. Not Roosevelt. And why?

Why? Why did they — an enormous, a heterogeneous *they* — distrust him so much? With an emotional as well as an intellectual distrust whose echoes lived strong in England until the

gunfire drowned them out in the high summer of 'Forty, and
which was to flare up again, across the ocean, later in the war.
They, all, distrusted him because he was uncategorizable. He
was the kind of person whom mediocrities instinctively fear.
"He is not steady" said conservative respectability. "He is a reactionary" said progressive intellectuality. But at the bottom
the sources of their distrust were much the same. Neville
Chamberlain and Eleanor Roosevelt, Harold Laski and Edward Stettinius distrusted Churchill out of the same human
motives. He did not have the kind of intellect that has a natural
appeal to Overseers of Harvard University and to deans of
women's colleges in New England. At the time when Churchill
began to sputter against the Hitler German danger he was dismissed not only by the stolid dumbness of the Baldwin and
Chamberlain supporters; it was at that time that Harold Laski
wrote that Hitler was not much more than a tool in the hands
of German capitalism, it was at that time that Alger Hiss was
the chief adviser of the Nye Committee, investigating the mis-
deeds of British militarism left over from the First World War;
ten years later the same Hiss was to sit on Roosevelt's right
at the Yalta table, with his long ambitious Quaker face, that
intellectual mug, calculating, self-conscious, and smug.

"A splendid anachronism," wrote a British intellectual in
one of the Sunday papers, trying to reconstruct his attitude
toward Churchill during the war. Who were — and who are —
the peddlers of anachronisms, the real reactionaries? Were
they not those who believed (and who still believe) that history
is a process of vast economic developments, who predicted
that Hitler could not wage war because, as statistics proved,

he would run out of oil or tin or rubber in a few weeks, the same people who had thought beforehand that his government would not last in face of the Concerted Opposition of the German Working Class? Wasn't it Churchill rather who immediately understood that Hitler was a very modern incarnation of a very old evil, Churchill who almost always knew instinctively what it was that was really new and what it was that was really old?

A man by the name of Henry Fairlie wrote in the *Sunday Telegraph:* "Mr A. J. P. Taylor said last week that historians of the future would ignore at their peril the spiritual contact which one man found in 1940 with the rest of his fellow-countrymen. . . . If Mr Taylor is not afraid to talk of a 'spiritual contact,' I see no reason why one should be afraid to talk of a vision." "Afraid" is good. For God's sake, why should one be *afraid* to admit the existence of something that was a matter of spirit, something that was not a matter of "production" or, at that, of "opinion" statistics? This is no longer the outcome of racial shyness; it is a kind of perverted crampedness of mind. It is this belated triumph of Josiah Bounderby that had laid the spirit of England so low that Churchill had to come to lift it up at its greatest danger: this Bounderby philosophy which, bruited now in the name of Freud and of Marx (how curious it is that both of them are buried here in London), is again abroad in this land?

What remains then, for England, on this Sunday? The nervous tic on the face of the man when he ordered a Wimpy. The essential, the uneradicable reticence graven into the hearts of the girls and of the women of England even as they leaf through the latest sex book or magazine. This Sunday stillness.

At midday we went to Mass in a Roman Catholic church on High Street in Kensington. It was not a very attractive church, set back between the brown brick houses. It was full of people: a few Poles and in the pew ahead of us the earnest and solicitous heads of other Europeans, but the majority of the congregation was English, infinitely serious English men and women with their children. Living through the last phase of the Protestant episode, of the long unhappy chapter of Roman Catholicism in England, with the old suspicions and the mistrust melting away, with reconciliation setting in, these English Catholics, perhaps better than any other Catholics in the Western world, know what it means to be Christians in a post-Christian land.

In this people who ushered in the modern age there is still a mystical, a near-medieval strain, a strain that has been part and parcel of their Protestantism, of their Puritanism, of their Industrial Revolution, of their English socialism. It is there in this living strain of English Catholicism which, in the twentieth century — curious paradox in the spiritual history of England — has become one of the strongest subterranean streams of a peculiar Englishness. To be hounded by heaven was one way to put it — but it was not only the Gerard Manley Hopkinses who sensed this. Even Aleister Crowley. Or Malcolm Muggeridge. Hounded by the sense of Satan or of God in a new-old, postmodern way, preoccupied, unlike many other people in the Western civilization, with the haunting reality of the question of whence we have come and where we are to go. Even now.

Then to midday dinner in an English home; we sat in friendliness for a little while; after that the cold wind whipping the torn papers in the doorways; through the brown Sunday afternoon and the wide streets to the steel tower of the airways terminal, with its inscriptions in many tongues. In a foreign airplane we rose into the winter evening sky.

In the hot droning airplane the Sunday papers again. *His name. Churchill.* How the very sound and the shape of his name fitted him. Pouting, aristocratic, flecked by sunlight. The round and juicy sound of the first syllable, formed by lips curling to speak just as his, the air filling up the cheeks of a seventeenth-century boy with a young and churchy sound. The pout makes it human and humorous rather than churched (but, then, the sound of the English *church* is so much more attractive, rounder, than the high guttural Gothic of *Kirche,* than the cold Roman-law *église,* than the hard angular Celtic *kell*). The pout merges, in a genial way, into the second syllable. There is nothing chilly about that final syllable, it is short, shiny, even brilliant, that springy sound of a rill. The sound of the full name is serious and humorous: it has a male charm about it: it is like the baroque fountains of Blenheim. (English rather than British; an English name whose bearer is now buried in English earth; English earth with its Roman and Saxon and Norman layers; an English man who had a romantic and exaggerated, an expansive notion of Britishness perhaps precisely because he was neither Scottish nor Welsh.) The shape of the

name, too: like the shape of his body: compact, slightly corpulent, with the glimmer of a single jewel, jaunty. The fluted cy-
lindrical second portion giving clear form to the roundness of
the first. Wearing his black 1940 hat, he looked like that dome
of St. Paul's on occasion. Churchill. Churchill.